Proofs of the Existence of God

–

PROOFS OF THE EXISTENCE OF GOD

gleaned from revealed and inspired sources
with brief commentary

by Peter Terry

BOSTON • 2019

PROOFS OF THE EXISTENCE OF GOD
Compiled by Peter Terry

(Global Faith Book Series. Vol. 2)

Series Editor: Mikhail Sergeev, *University of the Arts (Philadelphia)*

ISBN 978-1950319053
Library of Congress Control Number 2019946608

Cover Image:
William Blake. *God Writing upon the Tables of the Covenant*
National Galleries of Scotland. William Findlay Watson Bequest 1881

Published by M·GRAPHICS PUBLISHING
☐ www.mgraphics-publishing.com
✉ info@mgraphics-publishing.com
   mgraphics.books@gmail.com

Printed in the U.S.A.

Contents

"In the beginning, God..." This has been the belief of most of our ancestors, for the better part of three millennia. For several centuries though, there have been doubters, and, in response to the doubters, there have been attempts to prove the existence of God. We will examine the response to these doubters in the divine philosophy[1] of Bahá'u'lláh (1817–1892) and his son, 'Abdu'l-Bahá (1844–1921), both born in Iran and deceased in the Holy Land. In most cases we will be citing statements by 'Abdu'l-Bahá, unless otherwise noted. In order to give the reader an intellectual context in which to consider these arguments, other proofs will be cited here, some of them ancient, and others of more recent provenance.

We may well ask, for whom are these proofs? One answer to this question is as follows:

> "People are divided into two sections, one which is satisfied with the knowledge of the attributes of divinity, and the other which strives to establish the existence of divinity, and be informed of the fundamental principles of divine philosophy."[2]

This answer points to two temperaments, the one satisfied with tradition and the other demanding proof. Another answer

---

[1] Divine philosophy (*hikmat ilahi* in Persian and *hikmat al-ilahiyyat* in Arabic) is a term used widely by Bahá'u'lláh and 'Abdu'l-Bahá to denote philosophical theology and the wisdom and knowledge of God as revealed by the Manifestation of God and his chosen ones.

[2] *Star of the West* [SW], VI:8, 62. This statement and others cited from *Star of the West* are reported utterances of 'Abdu'l-Bahá.

points to those who are satisfied with another kind of status quo, the status quo of scientific consensus and sensory experience:

> "The materialist comes to the conclusion that life in other words means composition; that wherever we find single elements combined in aggregate form there we behold the phenomena of organic life; that every organic composition is organic life. Now if life means composition of elements then the materialist may come to the conclusion of the non-necessity of a creator; for composition is all there is to it, and that is accomplished by adhesion or cohesion."[3]

Proofs of the existence of God are for those who strive "to establish the existence of divinity, and be informed of the fundamental principles of divine philosophy",[4] to those who are already convinced of the existence of God and wish to establish this existence upon firm and enduring philosophical foundations; and for those who will reject the existence of God if they are not convinced otherwise.

We initially discovered three varieties of proofs for the existence of God—"rational" (logical, scientific) proofs[5]; "scriptural proofs from the Old and New Testaments or the Qur'an"[6]; and "spiritual proofs".[7] We propose that there are also sensory proofs for the existence of God, and our first Chapter is devoted to these. The Scriptural proofs are known to believers and rejected by unbelievers and hence of lesser significance and effect. It is acknowledged in the Epistemology of 'Abdu'l-Bahá that inasmuch as scripture and other religious traditions are interpreted by way

---

[3] *The Promulgation of Universal Peace* [PUP], pp. 421–25
[4] *Bahai Scriptures* [BS], #594, p. 290; alternate translation in *'Abdu'l-Bahá on Divine Philosophy* [ABDP], p. 104
[5] SAQ I:1–3; SW VI:3, 21–24; SW VI:8, 62–64; SWAB 46–71; SW XIV:4, 101–109
[6] BS #595, p. 290; SW VI:8, 62; ABDP p. 104
[7] SAQ I:14; PUP 425; SW VI:8, 64; SW XIV:4, 108–109

of the intellect, that they serve as an adjunct criterion to the criterion of reason.

While the intellect is not regarded as an infallible source of truth, in the case of proofs for the existence of God it seems to be the best suited to contemporary man:

> "These are rational arguments, which are what the people of the world require in this day."[8]

However, these rational proofs are not necessary for those who have become illumined with the Divine Light—they have no need of rational proofs:

> "These are theoretical arguments adduced for weak souls, but if the eye of inner vision be opened, a hundred thousand clear proofs will be seen. Thus, when man feels the indwelling spirit, he is in no need of arguments for its existence; but for those who are deprived of the grace of the spirit, it is necessary to set forth external arguments."[9]

Likewise (and for references see the above cited list for spiritual proofs), the following quotations are pertinent:

> "I ask God that His confirmations may encompass you; that your hearts may become radiant; that your eyes may become illumined through witnessing the signs of God; that your ears hearken to the anthems of heaven; that your faces be set aglow with the radiant light of the word of God..."[10]

> "Thank God that He has given you such a power through which you can comprehend these divine mysteries. Reflect deeply, ponder carefully, think minutely, and

---

[8] SAQ I:3.2
[9] SAQ I:2.8
[10] SW VI:3, p. 24; reprint in PUP 425

then the doors of knowledge shall be opened unto you..."[11]

"The merciful outpourings of that Divine Essence, however, are vouchsafed unto all beings and it is incumbent upon man to ponder in his heart upon the effusions of the Divine Grace, the soul (of man) being counted as one (sign of it), rather than upon the Divine Essence itself. This is the utmost limit of human understanding."[12]

This compilation and commentary has been assembled over the course of several years by myself, with assistance from a number of authors[13] and discussants, all of us fellow seekers after truth.

---

[11] SW VI:8, p. 64

[12] SW XIV:4, 108; reprinted as *Tablet to Dr. Forel*, p. 25

[13] See bibliography for complete listing of books and websites, including http://www.peterkreeft.com/topics-more/20_arguments-gods-existence.htm

CHAPTER ONE

SENSORY PROOFS
OF THE EXISTENCE OF GOD

The world of nature is that world which we perceive through our senses. While human beings are certain endowed with fine sensory organs, the faculties of sensory perception are surely possessed by animals to a superlative degree, and, for 'Abdu'l-Bahá, the

> "pathway of nature is the pathway of the animal realm. The animal acts in accordance with the requirements of nature, follows its own instincts and desires. Whatever its impulses and proclivities may be, it has the liberty to gratify them; yet it is a captive of nature. It cannot deviate in the least degree from the road nature has established... it is a captive of the senses and deprived of that which lies beyond them. It is subject to what the eye sees, the ear hears, the nostrils sense, the taste detects and touch reveals. These sensations are acceptable and sufficient for the animal."[14] "As to the animal: It is endowed only with sense perception... That is to say, the animal in its creation is a captive of the senses. Beyond the tangibilities and impressions of the senses it cannot accept anything."[15]

Hence, in the animal we have a creature which is entirely informed by the senses.

---

[14] PUP 177
[15] PUP 357

5

Does the animal have the capacity to think abstractly and to know intellectually as does man? 'Abdu'l-Bahá answers in the negative:

"The animal possesses no power of ideation or conscious intelligence..."[16] "The animal cannot apprehend ideal realities. The animal cannot conceive of the earth as a sphere. The intelligence of an animal located in Europe could never have planned the discovery of the continent of America. The animal kingdom is incapable of discovering the latent mysteries of nature—such as electricity—and bringing them forth from the invisible plane to the plane of visibility. It is evident that the discoveries and inventions transcend the animal intelligence...the bestowals of abstract reason and intellect are absent in its endowment. That is the say, the animal in its creation is a captive of the senses. Beyond the tangibilities and impressions of the senses it cannot accept anything. It denies everything. It is incapable of ideal perception and, therefore, a captive of the senses."[17]

Does the animal know of the existence of God? 'Abdu'l-Bahá answers again in the negative:

"It is utterly lacking spiritual susceptibilities, ignorant of divine religion and without knowledge of the Kingdom of God...that which is beyond the range of the senses, that realm of phenomena through which the conscious pathway to the Kingdom of God leads, the world of spiritual susceptibilities and divine religion—of these the animal is completely unaware, for in its highest station it is a captive of nature...the animal is absolutely ignorant of the realm of spirit and out of touch with the inner world of conscious realization...it is entirely bereft of that which lies beyond,

---

[16] PUP 177
[17] PUP 357

absolutely oblivious of the Kingdom of God and its traces, whereas God has deposited within the human creature an illimitable power by which he can rule the world of nature."[18] "The animals are without knowledge of God; so to speak, they are deniers of Divinity and understanding nothing of the Kingdom, they are utterly ignorant of spiritual things and uninformed of the supernatural world."[19]

'Abdu'l-Bahá does not claim that all created things, that all things in existence know God, perceive God, or even are aware of the existence of God. This perception is a peculiar attribute of the human world.

'Abdu'l-Bahá now describes the materialists in this fashion:

"One of the strangest things witnessed is that the materialists of today are proud of their natural instincts and bondage. They state that nothing is entitled to belief and acceptance except that which is sensible or tangible. By their own statements they are captives of nature, unconscious of the spiritual world, uninformed of the divine Kingdom and unaware of heavenly bestowals. If this be a virtue, the animal has attained to it to a superlative degree... The animal would agree with the materialist in denying the existence of that which transcends the senses. If we admit that being limited to the plane of the senses is a virtue, the animal is indeed more virtuous than man, for it is entirely bereft of that which lies beyond..."[20] "Therefore, if it be a perfection and virtue to be without knowledge of God and His Kingdom, the animals have attained the highest degree of excellence and proficiency."[21]

---

[18] PUP 177
[19] PUP 262
[20] PUP 177
[21] PUP 262

In referring to a visit to the city of Paris, 'Abdu'l-Bahá states that "most of the scholars, professors and learned men proved to be materialists."[22] Likewise, after visiting cities in the United States, 'Abdu'l-Bahá noted that

"In cities like New York the people are submerged in the sea of materialism. Their sensibilities are attuned to material forces, their perceptions purely physical. The animal energies predominate in their activities; all their thoughts are directed to material things; day and night they are devoted to the attractions of this world, schools and temples of learning knowledge of the sciences acquired is based upon material observations only; there is no realization of Divinity in their methods and conclusions—all have reference to the world of matter. They are not interested in attaining knowledge of the mysteries of God or understanding the secrets of the heavenly Kingdom; what they acquire is based altogether upon visible and tangible evidences. Beyond these evidences they are without susceptibilities; they have no idea of the world of inner significances and are utterly out of touch with God, considering this an indication of reasonable attitude and philosophical judgment whereof they are self-sufficient and proud."[23]

Whether in Europe or in America,

"some of the sagacious men declare: We have attained to the superlative degree of knowledge; we have penetrated the laboratory of nature, studying sciences and arts; we have attained the highest station of knowledge in the human world; we have investigated the facts as they are and have arrived at the conclusion that nothing is rightly acceptable except the tangible, which alone is

[22] PUP 16
[23] PUP 261–262

a reality worthy of credence; all that is not tangible is imagination and nonsense."[24]

In addressing these scholars, philosophers, scientists and other learned men, the argument of 'Abdu'l-Bahá is carried to its inevitable conclusion:

"In fact, from this standpoint the animal is the greater philosopher because it is completely ignorant of the Kingdom of God, possesses no spiritual susceptibilities and is uninformed of the heavenly world."[25]

"Then the donkey is the greatest scientist and the cow an accomplished naturalist, for they have obtained what they know without schooling and years of laborious study in colleges, trusting implicitly to the evidence of the senses and relying solely upon intuitive virtues. The cow, for instance, is a lover of the visible and a believer in the tangible, contented and happy when pasture is plenty, perfectly serene, a blissful exponent of the transcendental school of philosophy. Such is the status of the material philosophers, who glory in sharing the condition of the cow, imagining themselves in a lofty station."[26]

"The animal lives this kind of life blissfully and untroubled, whereas the material philosophers labor and study for ten or twenty years in schools and colleges, denying God, the Holy Spirit and divine inspirations. The animal is even a greater philosopher, for it attains the ability to do this without labor and study. For instance, the cow denies God and the Holy Spirit, knows nothing of divine inspirations, heavenly bounties or spiritual emotions

---

[24] PUP 360–361
[25] PUP 179
[26] PUP 262

and is stranger to the world of hearts. Like the philosophers, the cow is the captive of nature and knows nothing beyond the range of the senses."[27]

"Strange indeed that after twenty years training in colleges and universities man should reach such a station wherein he will deny the existence of the ideal or that which is not perceptible to the senses. Have you ever stopped to think that the animal already has graduated from such a university? Have you ever realized that the cow is already a professor emeritus of that university? For the cow without hard labor and study is already a philosopher of the superlative degree in the school of nature. The cow denies everything that is not tangible, saying, 'I can see! I can eat! Therefore, I believe only in that which is tangible!' Then why should we go to the colleges? Let us go to the cow."[28]

Everything that we perceive through the instrumentalities of our senses which is a creation of God is a revelation of the signs and attributes of that Unknowable Essence. Does this mean that everything that exists is a revelation of the attributes of God? On some level, of course. However, there is a vast difference between what God has created and what man may have done with that creation. What man may have done with a particular creation of God certainly reveals attributes of God firstly inasmuch as that creation reveals attributes of God in any condition, and secondly, that man demonstrates certain of those attributes in manipulating natural phenomena—it is through the gift of God that man has this power, possessed by no other of His creations, and one of the reasons why man is described as "created in the image of God". However, it may be more difficult to discern or even to affirm that perfections of God are directly revealed in whatever man does with God's creations—for man may make

---

[27] PUP 311–312
[28] PUP 361

something ugly and harmful out of what was originally beautiful and harmless.

Man's freedom of choice is a sign of God but man's every choice is not necessarily a sign of God in itself, for man may turn either towards God or away from Him, and if man turns away from God that act does not directly reveal the attributes of God at the same level as his turning towards God. Or does it? Man, in virtually every culture and civilization, has believed in a divine power, and in many cases has multiplied that divine power even to the point of believing that it animated every phenomenon of nature and many phenomena of human experience. Divine philosophy certainly affirms the spirit in all beings, in the mineral, the vegetable, the animal, the human, the prophets, the afterlife, dreams, visions, and beyond all of these phenomena, the Unknowable Essence. Many human beings, perhaps human beings generally have experiences, often triggered by specific sensory perceptions such as sunrises or sunsets, climbing to the summits of hills or mountains, coming to the banks of a river or the shores of a sea, witnessing a meteor shower or an eclipse or a volcanic eruption or a migrating flock of birds, which impel us to a feeling of gratitude for the gift of life or a feeling of awe and wonder at the miraculous beauty and variety of the world we inhabit. At such moments, at least some individuals feel that God must exist. Is this a sensory proof of the existence of God? Of course not. It is an intuitive response to a sensory experience, a convergence of highly pleasurable sensory impulses with sentimental memory significances. This perception of supernatural beauty or of the miraculous will be treated in the section devoted to spiritual proofs. Many of the rational, traditional and spiritual proofs for the existence of God can be perceived to some degree by the senses, but none of these proofs proceed from sensory experience unassisted.

Divine philosophy[29] considers that the criterion of the senses and the perception of the senses and hence pure and simple the

---

[29] Please see footnote #1 if you missed or want to be reminded of the definition of divine philosophy.

sensing of the world of nature are not operable in the realm of the spirit, the intellect, the ideal, religion, the afterlife, and in the knowledge of God.

> "When thou dost carefully consider this matter, thou wilt see that a lower plane can never comprehend a higher. The mineral kingdom, for example, which is lower, is precluded from comprehending the vegetable kingdom; for the mineral, any such understanding would be utterly impossible. In the same way, no matter how far the vegetable kingdom may develop, it will achieve no conception of the animal kingdom, and any such comprehension at its level would be unthinkable, for the animal occupieth a plane higher than that of the vegetable: this tree cannot conceive of hearing and sight. And the animal kingdom, no matter how far it may evolve, can never become aware of the reality of the intellect, which discovereth the inner essence of all things, and comprehendeth those realities which cannot be seen; for the human plane as compared with that of the animal is very high. And although these beings all co-exist in the contingent world, in each case the difference in their stations precludeth their grasp of the whole; for no lower degree can understand a higher, such comprehension being impossible."[30]

The mineral cannot know God. The vegetable cannot know God. The animal cannot know God. How is it possible that man can know God, Who occupies a plane infinitely exalted above that of human existence and consciousness? This is not merely a question of appropriate and possible instrumentalities but an essential existential problem. We must seek the solution thereto before resuming our investigation of the proofs for the existence of God.

---

[30] SWAB 46

'Abdu'l-Bahá attests that

> "two kinds of knowledge: the knowledge of the essence of a thing and the knowledge of its attributes. The essence of each thing is known only through its attributes; otherwise, that essence is unknown and unfathomed. As our knowledge of things, even of created and limited ones, is of their attributes and not of their essence, how then can it be possible to understand in its essence the unbounded Reality of the Divinity?"[31]

> "When we glance at all phenomena, we discover that the real identity of any given phenomenon is unknown. Phenomena or created objects are known only by their attributes. Man discerns only manifestations or attributes of objects, whereas the reality or identity of them is unknown to him. For example, this flower—what do we understand by this flower? We understand the qualities apparent and appertaining to this flower; but the very elemental reality or identity of the flower remains unknown to us. As regards its external appearance and attributes, these are knowable; but as regards the inner being, the very identity, it is unknown. Now so long as earthly phenomena are unknown as regards their identity, and are known only through their properties or qualities, how much more is this true concerning the reality of divinity, that holy reality which cannot be comprehended by any human grasp?"[32]

Divine philosophy asserts categorically that man is incapable of knowing the essence of any thing, of the mineral, the vegetable, the animal, the human, and hence certainly of the divine. Man can only know through the observation and understanding of attributes, qualities, manifestations of existences. How then is it possible for man to know God?

---

[31] SAQ I:59.3–4
[32] PUP 421

"Then how could it be possible for a contingent reality, that is, man, to understand the nature of that pre-existent Essence, the Divine Being? The difference in station between man and the Divine Reality is thousands upon thousands of times greater than the difference between the vegetable and animal. And that which the human being would conjure up in his mind is but the fanciful image of his human condition, it doth not encompass God's reality but rather is encompassed by it. That is, man graspeth his own illusory conceptions, but the Reality of Divinity can never be grasped: It, Itself, encompasseth all created things, and all created things are in Its grasp. That Divinity which man doth imagine for himself exsiteth only in his mind, not in truth. Man, however, existeth both in his mind and in truth; thus man is greater than that fanciful reality which he is able to imagine. The furthermost limits of this bird of clay are these: he can flutter along for some short distance, into the endless vast; but he can never soar upward to the Sun in the high heavens."[33]

"Know then: that divinity which other communions and peoples have conjured up, falleth within the scope of their imagination, and not beyond it, whereas the reality of the Godhead is beyond all conceiving."[34]

The reader may well be astonished to encounter such an argument in a text devoted to divine philosophy! That reader may well be disturbed that such a frank and fearless discussion should come so early in a voluminous work of this nature. This would appear to many of you as a classic description of the agnostic or even of the atheist position, similar in many regards to the propositions of Ludwig Feuerbach himself. The purpose of 'Abdu'l-Bahá in stating such a position is simply to acknowledge the truth that

---

[33] SWAB 46–47
[34] SWAB 50–51

all existing concepts of God are limited to the minds which have conceived of them, and have less claim to reality by far than their creators, human beings. The old "god" or "gods" are dead, meaningless, false. While some thinkers have stopped here, 'Abdu'l-Bahá continues:

> "That which comes within human grasp is finite, and we are infinite in relation thereto because we can grasp it. Assuredly the finite is lesser than the infinite; the infinite is ever greater."[35]

> "In short, the point is this that the world of man is supernatural in its relation to the vegetable kingdom, though in reality it is not so. Relatively to the plant, the reality of man, his power of hearing and sight, are all supernatural, and for the plant to comprehend that reality and the nature of the powers of man's mind is impossible."[36]

This would also appear to buttress the agnostic and atheist in their unbelief. However, 'Abdu'l-Bahá proceeds to point out that

> "all created things are limited, and this very limitation of all beings proveth the reality of the Limitless; for the existence of a limited being denoteth the existence of a Limitless One."[37]

This assertion will be carefully examined in a subsequent section, one pertaining to the logical, rational, reasoned, scientific arguments for the existence of God.

> "The question was, 'What is the Reality of Divinity, or what do we understand by God?'...'How shall we know God?' We know Him by His attributes. We know Him by His signs. We know Him by His names...If we wish to come in touch with the reality of divinity, we do so by

---

[35] PUP 421–422
[36] SW XIV:4, 108–109
[37] SWAB 50

recognizing its phenomena, its attributes and traces which are widespread in the universe. All things in the world of phenomena are expressive of that one reality. Its lights are shining, its heat is manifest, its power is expressive and its education or training resplendent everywhere. What proof could there be greater than that of its functioning, or its attributes which are manifest?"[38] "It is clear, then, that the reality of God is revealed in His perfections…"[39] "How then can the reality of man which is accidental, ever comprehend the Reality of God which is eternal? It is self-evidently an impossibility. Hence we can observe the traces and attributes of God which are resplendent in all phenomena and shining as the sun at midday, and know surely that these emanate from an infinite source."[40]

"As to the Holy Manifestations of God, They are the focal points where the signs, tokens and perfections of that sacred, pre-existent Reality appear in all their splendour… the Sun of Truth dwelleth in a sky to which no soul hath any access, and which no mind can reach, and He is far beyond the comprehension of all creatures."[41] "In like manner for man to comprehend the Divine Essence and the nature of the great Hereafter is in no wise possible. The merciful outpourings of that Divine Essence, however, are vouchsafed unto all beings and it is incumbent upon man to ponder in his heart upon the effusions of the Divine Grace, the soul (of man) being counted as one (sign of it), rather than upon the Divine Essence itself. This is the utmost limit for human understanding."[42]

---

[38] PUP 422
[39] SWAB 51
[40] PUP 422–423
[41] SWAB 51
[42] SW XIV:4, 348; reprint in *Tablet to Dr. Forel*, p. 25

"The invisible realm of the Divinity is sanctified and exalted above the comprehension of all beings, and all that can be imagined is mere human understanding. The power of human understanding does not encompass the reality of the divine Essence: All that man can hope to achieve is to comprehend the attributes of the Divinity, the light of which is manifest and resplendent in the world and within the souls of men."[43]

How then are human beings to know God?

"When we examine the world and the souls of men, the perspicuous signs of the perfections of the Divinity appear clear and manifest, for the realities of all things attest to the existence of a universal Reality."[44]

Man can discern the attributes, the perfections of God in all created things. This is the first assertion, and a challenging one certainly, in view of the previous statements regarding the inability of the animal and the physical man to perceive Divinity, and the inability of the intellectual man to conceive of any "god" but the "idol" of his own creation.

"The reality of the Divinity is even as the sun, which from the heights of its sanctity shines upon every land, and of whose radiance every land and every soul receives a share. Were it not for this light and this radiance, nothing could exist."[45]

Are these attributes, these perfections of God which are revealed in all of God's creations, are they actually the attributes of God?

"As it hath previously been mentioned, these attributes and perfections that we recount of the Divine Essence,

---

[43] SAQ I:59.7
[44] SAQ I:59.8
[45] SAQ I:59.8

these we have derived from the existence and observation of beings, and it is not that we have comprehended the Essence and perfection of God. When we say that the Divine Essence understandeth and is free, we do not mean that we have discovered the Divine Will and Purpose, but rather that we have acquired knowledge of them through the Divine Grace revealed and manifested in the realities of things."[46]

Hence, 'Abdu'l-Bahá asserts that the perfections of God by which God is known by human beings are those perfections as they are revealed in all created things through the operation of the Divine Grace. What is this Divine Grace? The Divine Grace, the Divine Revelation are the Holy Spirit, the appearance of which is most complete in the Holy Manifestations of God.

"Now, all created things tell of this light, partake of its rays, and receive their portion thereof, but the full splendour of the perfections, bounties, and attributes of the Divinity shines forth from the reality of the Perfect Man, that is, that unique Individual Who is the universal Manifestation of God. For the other beings have each received only a portion of that light, but the universal Manifestation of God is the mirror held before this Sun, and the latter manifests itself therein with all its perfections, attributes, signs, and effects. The knowledge of the reality of the Divinity is in no wise possible, but the knowledge of the Manifestations of God is the knowledge of God, for the bounties, splendours, and attributes of God are manifest in Them. Thus, whoso attains to the knowledge of the Manifestations of God attains to the knowledge of God, and whoso remains heedless of Them remains bereft of that knowledge."[47]

---

[46] SW XIV:4, 108–109
[47] SAQ I:59.8–9

The "First Intellect" or "Primal Will" which "appeareth resplendent in every Prophet and speaketh forth in every revealed Book"[48] is not identical to God Himself.

> "Though the First Intellect is without beginning, this does not mean that it shares in the preexistence of God, for in relation to the existence of God the existence of that universal Reality is mere nothingness—it cannot even be said to exist, let alone to partake of the pre-existence of God."[49] "Yet the Holy Manifestations of God are even as a looking-glass, burnished and without stain, which gathereth streams of light out of that Sun, and then scattereth the glory over the rest of creation. In that polished surface, the Sun with all Its majesty standeth clearly revealed. Thus, should the mirrored Sun proclaim, 'I am the Sun!' this is but truth; and should It cry, 'I am not the Sun!' this is the truth as well. And although the Day-Star, with all Its glory, Its beauty, Its perfections, be clearly visible in that mirror without stain, still It hath not come down from Its own lofty station in the realms above, It hath not make Its way into the mirror; rather doth It continue to abide, as It will forever, in the supernal heights of Its own holiness."[50]

To recapitulate then, in divine philosophy we find the realization that the concepts of God current and historical are the idols of our own imaginings. We find that we can only know the attributes of things, not the things in themselves. We find that our senses do not inform us of the existence of God. Hence, 'Abdu'l-Bahá has effectively devalued the traditional crutches for belief in God—the images which we have conceived of for ourselves or imitated from our families and neighbors; the fancy that some of us had that we understood the essence of reality, to which we

---

[48] SWB 126
[49] SAQ I:53.6
[50] SWAB 50

gave the name "God"; the contemporary conviction that we can perceive through our senses everything that really and truly exists and that any existence outside of such sensory perception is purely imaginary. What then are our fancies and misapprehensions replaced by? A firm and fearless affirmation that the attributes, the perfections of God are revealed in all of His creations, that we can know these attributes by studying those creations, that we cannot know the essence of God or anything else about God save His attributes, and furthermore, that the perfect Manifestation of those attributes is accessible to each one of us. That Manifestation of God is found in human history, in the person of the founders of most of the established religions.

Divine philosophy might have left us all to our own devises at this point. After all, having been told that God was revealed in His creations and in His Manifestations, we might be expected to investigate the two by studying the "nature" of the phenomena in this universe, and by looking into the traces of the prophet-founders of religions. Divine philosophy does not abandon the seeker for truth however. Rather, stunned, confused, skeptical, perhaps even disappointed, we are advised that we have just begun the voyage, that this is a long trip and we must be patient and attentive.

CHAPTER TWO

REASON, LOGIC AND SCIENCE DEFINED

'Abdu'l-Bahá does not regard the way of the senses as a reliable standard for investigating the existence of God. As indicated earlier, his epistemology refers to four human standards, and the first of these is that of reason, of logic, of science. All three of these concepts are related to the functioning of the human mind or intellect, an attribute and power which makes man distinct from the animal kingdom.[51]

> "Man is distinguished above the animals through his reason. The perceptions of man are of two kinds: tangible, or sensible, and reasonable, whereas the animal perceptions are limited to the senses, the tangible only...As to the animal: It is endowed only with sense perception. It is lacking the reasonable perception...Virtue, or perfection, belongs to man, who possesses both the capacity of the senses and ideal perception."[52]

What then do we understand by these words, "reason", "logic", and "science"? In search of uses of these words which will be recognizable to all readers of English as well as related to the author of these proofs, the definitions consulted are from a dictionary,[53] an encyclopedia,[54] and the writings and discourses of

---

[51] PUP 356–357
[52] PUP 357
[53] *The Oxford Universal Dictionary on Historical Principles* [OUD], 3rd edition. Oxford: Clarendon Press, 1955
[54] *The International Cyclopaedia* [IC], A compendium of human knowledge. New York: Dodd, Mead & Co., 1898

'Abdu'l-Bahá. We will begin with "reason", inasmuch as it seems to be the most seminal and comprehensive of the three.

REASON

"III. 1. That intellectual power or faculty (usu. regarded as characteristic of mankind...) which is ordinarily employed in adapting thought or action to some end; the guiding principle of the human mind in the process of thinking... IV. 1. The act of reasoning or argumentation. 2. Consideration, regard, respect. 3. Way, manner, method spec. the method of a science."[55]

"The word reason denotes that function of our intelligence having reference to the attainment of a particular class of truths. We know a great many things by immediate or actual experience. Our senses tell us that we are thirsty, that we hear a sound, that we are affected by light. These facts are truths of sense, or of immediate knowledge, and do not involve the reason. Reason comes into play when we know a thing not immediately, but by some indirect process; as when, from seeing a river unusually swollen, we believe that there have been heavy rains at its sources. Here the mere sense tells us only that the river is high; it is by certain transitions of thought, or by the employment of our thinking powers, that we come to know the other circumstance, that in a remote part of the country there have been heavy rains. In ascertaining these truths of reason, or of inference, as they are called, there are various steps or operations, described under different names. Thus we have (1) DEDUCTION, or SYLLOGISM; (2) INDUCTION; and (3) GENERALIZATION of notions,

[55] OUD 1667

of which ABSTRACTION and DEFINITION are various phases."[56]

"Man is distinguished above the animals through his reason. The perceptions of man are of two kinds: tangible, or sensible, and reasonable, whereas the animal perceptions are limited to the senses, the tangible only. The tangible perceptions may be likened to this candle, the reasonable perceptions to the light. Calculations of mathematical problems and determining the spherical form of the earth are through the reasonable perceptions. The center of gravity is a hypothesis of reason. Reason itself is not tangible, perceptible to the senses. Reason is an intellectual verity or reality. All qualities are ideal realities, not tangible realities. For instance, we say this man is a scholarly man. Knowledge is an ideal attainment not perceptible to the senses. When you see this scholarly man, your eye does not see his knowledge, your ear cannot hear his science, nor can you sense it by taste. It is not a tangible verity."[57]

"The philosophers of the East consider the perfect criterion to be reason or intellect, and according to that standard the realities of all objects can be proved; for, they say, the standard of reason and intellect is perfect, and everything provable through reason is veritable. Therefore, these philosophers consider all philosophical deductions to be correct when weighed according to the standard of reason, and they state that the senses are the assistants and instruments of reason, and that although the investigation of realities may be conducted through the senses, the standard of knowing and judgment is reason itself."[58]

---

[56] IC 459–460
[57] PUP 357
[58] PUP 356

These sources regard "reason" as characteristic of man and not an endowment of the mineral, vegetable or animal kingdoms. They also agree that "reason" constitutes the intellectual faculty and the particular manner in which it functions. They distinguish between sensory perception and reasoning, and they identify reason with philosophy, science and disciplined thinking in general.

LOGIC

"1. The branch of philosophy that treats of the forms of thinking in general, and esp. of inference and scientific method."[59]

"This name denotes the science connected with the forms and methods of reasoning, and the establishment of truth by evidence. The science has come down to us from the Greeks, obtaining in great part the shape that we find it in from Aristotle, although he did not apply to it the name 'logic.' This name, signifying originally both thought and the expression of thought, must have been applied soon after the time of Aristotle...The definition of logic has never been, till lately, a matter of serious controversy. There was formerly a substantial unanimity, with some variations in the form of the phraseology employed. We find it called usually the art of reasoning, or the science of reasoning, or both the one and the other. And by reasoning has been always understood formal reasoning; that is, inferences stated in such general language that they apply to all kinds of matter alike, as when in arithmetic we say three times four is twelve, without considering what the numbers are numbers of...Mr. John Stuart Mill has propounded a radical innovation in the definition and province of

[59] OUD 1162

this subject. According to him, logic 'is the science of the operations of the understanding which are subservient to the estimation of evidence; both the process itself of proceeding from known truths to unknown, and all other intellectual operations in so far as auxiliary to this. It includes, therefore, the operation of naming; for language is an instrument of thought, as well as a means of communicating our thoughts. It includes also, definition and classification.' This definition has the merit of setting distinctly forth the end of the science, which is the essential point in every practical science, as logic is. That end is the estimation of evidence; in other words, it is not the ascertainment of all truth, but of those portions of truth that are authenticated by means of other truths, or by inference...inference is admitted on all hands to be of two kinds—deductive or formal inference, and inductive or real inference."[60]

"Today the logic and philosophy of Aristotle are known throughout the world."[61]

"The second criterion is that of the intellect, which was the principal criterion of comprehension for those pillars of wisdom, the ancient philosophers. They deduced things through the power of the mind and relied on rational arguments: All their arguments are based upon reason. But despite this, they diverged greatly in their opinions. They would even change their own views: For twenty years they would deduce the existence of something through rational arguments, and then afterwards they would disprove the same, again through rational arguments. Even Plato at first proved through rational arguments the immobility of the earth and the movement of the sun, and then subsequently established,

---

[60] IC IX:133
[61] PUP 327

again through rational arguments, the centrality of the sun and the movement of the earth."[62]

These sources agree that "logic" is the instrument of philosophy, and the method of reasoning. 'Abdu'l-Bahá does not go into details, while the other two sources identify logic with "inference", and the first source calls logic "a branch of philosophy" while the second source calls it "a science". The second and third sources refer to the ancient Greek foundations of logic, and the first and third sources to the relationship between logic and philosophy. "Philosophy" has been defined by our three sources in the Preface to this study, and the reader is referred thereto in the interests of abbreviation through non-repetition whenever possible. "Inference" will have to be defined, for otherwise we still do not know what "logic" means, with any precision.

INFERENCE

"1. The action or process of inferring; esp. in Logic, the forming of a conclusion from premises, either by induction or deduction; = Illation 1."[63]

"Induction... 7. Logic. The process of inferring a general law or principle from the observation of particular instances (opp. to deduction, q.v.); a conclusion derived from induction; formerly used in the wider sense of 'inference'."[64]

"Deduction... 5. The process of deducing from something known or assumed; spec. in Logic, inference by reasoning from generals to particulars."[65]

---

[62] SAQ V:83.3
[63] IC I:999
[64] IC I:994
[65] IC I:467

"Illation... 1. The action of drawing a conclusion from premises; hence, an inference, deduction, or conclusion."[66]

"But inference is admitted on all hands to be of two kinds—deductive or formal inference, and inductive or real inference. In the one, no more is inferred than is already contained in the premises; for example, 'All men are mortal, therefore the present generation of Englishmen will die,' is a formal inference; the conclusion is within, or less than, the premises. This is the kind of inference treated of in the deductive or syllogistic logic, which was till lately the whole of the science. In the other kind of inference, a conclusion is drawn wider than the premises, so that there is a real advance upon our knowledge: from certain things directly ascertained we infer other things that have not been ascertained by direct experiment, and which, but for such inference, we should have had to determine in that matter. Thus, 'This, that, and the other piece of matter, in which actual observations have been made, gravitates,' therefore, 'all inert matter, existing everywhere, known and unknown, gravitates,' is an inductive inference. Of this class of inferences, all the inductive sciences, including physics, chemistry, physiology, mental philosophy, etc., are made up."[67]

"Notwithstanding this, the philosophers of the West have certain syllogisms, or demonstrations, whereby they endeavor to prove that man had his origin in the animal kingdom; that although he is now a vertebrate, he originally lived in the sea; from thence he was transferred to the land and became vertebrate; that gradual-

---

[66] IC I:955
[67] IC IX:133

ly his feet and hands appeared in his anatomical development; then he began to walk on all fours, after which
he attained to human stature, walking erect. They find
that his anatomy has undergone successive changes, finally assuming human form, and that these intermedi-
ate forms or changes are like links connected. Between
man and the ape, however, there is one link missing, and
to the present time scientists have not been able to dis-
cover it. Therefore, the greatest proof of this Western
theory of human evolution is anatomical, reasoning
that there are certain vestiges of organs found in man
which are peculiar to the ape and lower animals, and
setting forth the conclusion that man at some time
in his upward progression has possessed these organs
which are no longer functioning but appear now as mere
rudiments and vestiges..."[68]

The definition of "logic" is now completed, inasmuch as not
only its historical and methodological context is now established,
but also its content is clearly delineated, composed, according to
the first and second authorities, of inference by deduction (syllogism) and by its opposite, induction; from generalities to particulars and from particulars to generalities. At the same time,
'Abdu'l-Bahá has asserted that "logic" may be used in demonstrating opposing hypotheses, that it is consequently to be accounted
valuable but not infallible.[69] We now come to the third term to be
defined: "science."

SCIENCE

"1. The state or fact of knowing... 2. Knowledge acquired by study... 3. A particular branch of knowledge
or study; a recognized department of learning... 4. A

---

[68] PUP 358
[69] Please see footnote #176.

branch of study which is concerned either with a connected body of demonstrated truths or with observed facts systematically classified and more or less colligated by being brought under general laws, and which includes trustworthy methods for the discovery of new truth within its own domain...5. The kind of knowledge or intellectual activity of which the 'sciences' are examples...In mod. use chiefly: The sciences (in sense 4) as dist. from other departments of learning; scientific doctrine or investigation."[70]

"Scientific... 4. Of an art, practice, operation, or method: Based upon or regulated by science, as opp. to mere traditional rules or empirical dexterity."[71]

"Sciences, the name for such portions of human knowledge as have been more or less generalized, systematized, and verified. Generality as opposed to mere particulars, system as opposed to random arrangement, and verification as opposed to looseness of assumption, concur in that superior kind of knowledge dignified by the title in question...The term philosophy (q.v.) is to a certain extent, but not altogether, coincident with science, being applied to the early efforts and strainings after the explanation of the universe, that preceded exact science in any department. Both names denote the pursuit of knowledge as knowledge, or for intellectual satisfaction, in contrast to the search that is limited to immediate practice or utility."[72]

"Science itself is an ideal verity."[73]

---

[70] IC I:1806
[71] Ibid.
[72] IC XIII:240
[73] PUP 357

"Man's inventions have appeared through the avenue of his reasonable faculties. All his scientific attainments have come through the faculty of reason."[74]

"On the other hand, it is evident and true, though most astounding, that in man there is present this super-natural force or faculty which discovers the realities of things and which possesses the power of idealization or intellection. It is capable of discovering scientific laws, and science we know is not a tangible reality. The mind itself, reason itself, is an ideal reality and not tangible."[75]

"Science is an effulgence of the Sun of Reality, the pow-er of investigating and discovering the verities of the universe, the means by which man finds a pathway to God."[76]

"Science is the first emanation from God toward man. All created beings embody the potentiality of material perfection, but the power of intellectual investigation and scientific acquisition is a higher virtue specialized to man alone. Other beings and organisms are deprived of this potentiality and attainment. God has created or deposited this love of reality in man. The development and progress of a nation is according to the measure and degree of that nation's scientific attainments. Through this means its greatness is continually increased, and day by day the welfare and prosperity of its people are assured. All blessings are divine in origin, but none can be compared with this power of intellectual investiga-tion and research, which is an eternal gift producing fruits of unending delight. Man is ever partaking of

---

[74] PUP 357–358
[75] PUP 360
[76] PUP 49

these fruits. All other blessings are temporary; this is an everlasting possession. Even sovereignty has its limitations and overthrow; this is a kingship and dominion which none can usurp or destroy. Briefly, it is an eternal blessing and divine bestowal, the supreme gift of God to man. Therefore, you should put forward your most earnest efforts toward the acquisition of science and arts. The greater your attainment, the higher your standard in the divine purpose. The man of science is perceiving and endowed with vision, whereas he who is ignorant and neglectful of this development is blind. The investigating mind is attentive, alive; the callous and indifferent mind is deaf and dead. A scientific man is a true index and representative of humanity, for through processes of INDUCTIVE REASONING[77] and RESEARCH he is informed of all that appertains to humanity, its status, conditions and happenings. He studies the human body politic, understands social problems and weaves the web and texture of civilization. In fact, science may be likened to a mirror wherein the infinite forms and images of existing things are revealed and reflected. It is the very foundation of all individual and national development. Without this basis of investigation, development is impossible. Therefore, seek with diligent endeavor the knowledge and attainment of all that lies within the power of this wonderful bestowal."[78]

Clearly then, what 'Abdu'l-Bahá defines and describes as "science" is much more comprehensive than either of the other authorities. For the first authority, "science" has meant historically any body of organized knowledge which is recognized as a "science", and this usage of the term is preserved for the modern classification of sciences. The second authority makes a similar state-

---

[77] Some words have been cited in BLOCK CAPITAL LETTERS for emphasis.

[78] PUP 49–50

ment, and relates modern "science" to that ancient philosophy which served as its precursor. It is left then for 'Abdu'l-Bahá to declare that "science" is divine in origin, that it is an "ideal reality", that it proceeds from another "ideal reality", the human power of investigation. For 'Abdu'l-Bahá, science is not merely the name of a body of organized knowledge, it is a spiritual endeavor, and the most essential occupation of human beings, the one which makes them distinct from animals and contributory to their own welfare and the progress of civilization. Science is not a man-made phenomenon—it is an endowment from God, and it is a revelation of the realities of things suitable to the capacity of man.

Western authorities define "science," as it has been used almost exclusively in the West during the past two centuries, in reference to the sciences of "mathematics, physics, chemistry, biology (vegetable and animal physiology), psychology (mind), sociology (society)... meteorology, mineralogy, botany, zoology, geology, also geography... astronomy... physics..."[79] and to which have been added anthropology, political science, economics, computer science and a number of other fields. These sciences are generally organized in two groupings, the one denominated "physical science" and the other "social science". 'Abdu'l-Bahá does not distinguish categories, classifications of subjects in the Western fashion. Divine philosophy includes in its definition of science both fundamental branches of traditional, historical and perennial philosophy—

> "Philosophy is of two kinds: natural and divine. Natural philosophy seeks knowledge of physical verities and explains material phenomena, whereas divine philosophy deals with ideal verities and phenomena of the spirit."[80] "Scientific knowledge is the highest attainment upon the human plane, for science is the discoverer of realities. It is of two kinds: material and spiritual. Material science is the investigation of nat-

[79] IC XIII:241
[80] PUP 326

ural phenomena; divine science is the discovery and realization of spiritual verities. The world of humanity must acquire both. A bird has two wings; it cannot fly with one. Material and spiritual science are the two wings of human uplift and attainment. Both are necessary—one the natural, the other supernatural; one material, the other divine. By the divine we mean the discovery of the mysteries of God, the comprehension of spiritual realities, the wisdom of God, inner significances of the heavenly religions and foundation of the law."[81] The "essence and fundamentals of" sciences, denoted as material and spiritual philosophy "have emanated from the Prophets."[82]

Now that terms have been identified and we understand what is meant by "reason", "logic", and "science" when these terms are employed by 'Abdu'l-Bahá, we will proceed with our study of rational proofs for the existence of God.

---

[81] PUP 138

[82] Baha'u'lláh. *Lawh-i-Hikmat*, in *Tablets of Baha'u'lláh* revealed after the Kitab-i-Aqdas (TB), p. 144

Chapter Three

Rational Proofs
of the Existence Of God

FIRST PROOF: COMPOSITION

Having already stated that the human being is incapable of understanding the essential nature of Deity, nor even of understanding His attributes except insofar as they are revealed in His creations, 'Abdu'l-Bahá proceeds to "set forth reasoned or inspired proofs as to the existence of the Divine Being, that is, proofs commensurate with the understanding of man."[83] What is the most efficacious sequence to present proofs? 'Abdu'l-Bahá states that

> "we must first present the rational arguments and only afterwards the spiritual ones."[84] "I will not quote to you the scriptural proofs from the Old and New Testaments and the Qur'an, for you are more or less familiar with those ideas... Therefore today I will speak to you of the proofs which establish scientifically the existence of God."[85]

When asked specifically: "Should we come in touch with those who are naturalists, or those who do not believe in God or His Prophets, how can we prove to them their Divinity?" 'Abdu'l-Bahá replied:

[83] SWAB 47
[84] SAQ IV:50.6
[85] BS #595, p. 290; SW VI:8, 62; ABDP, p. 104

"First of all, you should not argue with them or oppose them, or they will deny even the things which they see with their eyes. For example, they will see the light here, and they will say there is no light. One must talk to them very kindly, in order to let them know the desired object. When you ask them 'Who is the Creator of the world? What is your opinion in the matter?' They will answer: 'It is quite plain and evident that there are various kinds of elements, and by being composed a being is formed.' We must say, 'You are right, it seems to be so, but we have heard something else, some philosophers and learned men told us as follows...'"[86]

From thence begins an account of the argument of VOLUNTARY COMPOSITION.

The argument from composition was seemingly invented by the Islamic theologians called mutakalimun, the masters of kalam,[87] but it was revived and elaborated by 'Abdu'l-Bahá and then reformulated by William S. Hatcher.[88] There are four independent sources for this argument in the writings, talks and pilgrim's notes of 'Abdu'l-Bahá, and each will be quoted in full prior to any discussion, with the sources cited according to the detail of the description, from brief to detailed, beginning where we left off:

---

[86] Ida A. Finch, Alma and Fanny H. Knobloch. *Flowers culled from the Rose Garden of Acca.* 1908, p. 3 (These are the recollections of American believers of words uttered by 'Abdu'l-Bahá during their pilgrimage.)

[87] Herbert A. Davidson, *Proofs for Eternity, Creation and the Existence of God in Medieval Islamic and Jewish Philosophy.* New York: Oxford University Press, 1987, 146–153

[88] William S. Hatcher. *A Scientific Proof of the Existence of God,* The Journal of Bahá'í Studies, 5:4; *Prologue on Proving God, Causality, Composition, and the Origin of Existence and A Scientific Proof for the Existence of God,* in The Law of Love Enshrined: Selected Essays, Oxford: George Ronald, 1996, passim

SOURCE ONE

"When we look carefully at objects and things we can comprehend and understand that by the composition of some elements something is formed; this is quite evident. But there are three kinds of composition. One is accomplished by force; for instance, fire attracts water,[89] this is made through force—that is, the elements attract each other; when they come together they form an object. This kind of composition is called innate or natural attraction, made by force. The second kind of composition is said to be done by chance, for instance, it rained by chance, the sun cast its rays by chance; therefore, vegetables grow. The third is a composition made by will, by aim;—for instance,— A doctor gives a medicine which is composed of various elements, compounded by his will; knowing the ingredients of the drugs he compounds them by will. We must look and see very carefully that we understand whether the things or objects of the world are formed through the power of attraction made by force; if it is so, then there should not be the decomposition, because the elements attracted by the other must remain together everlastingly; corruption must not take place; some realize that there are both composition and decomposition. As to the second, which was by chance—this is also not perfect, but completely invalid. How can there be movement without a mover? As to the third, that all objects in the world are made or formed by will. Then, there should be a Creator for everything, for instance, to place the eye in its own place, the ear in its proper place, etc. Such a power creates, gives life to man, and works through His will. We

---

[89] The origin of this idea is found in the philosophy of Empedocles, an ancient Greek philosopher cited by Bahá'u'lláh and 'Abdu'l-Bahá. For more information see: https://en.wikipedia.org/wiki/Empedocles

call this will, God! All the prophets believed in such a Great Being."[90]

SOURCE TWO

"Now, formation is of three kinds and of three kinds only: ACCIDENTAL, NECESSARY, and VOLUNTARY. The coming together of the various constituent elements of beings cannot be accidental, for unto every effect there must be a cause. It cannot be compulsory, for then the formation must be an inherent property of the constituent parts and the inherent property of a thing can in nowise be dissociated from it, such as light that is the revealer of things, heat that causeth the expansion of elements and the (solar) rays which are the essential property of the sun.

"Thus under such circumstances the decomposition of any formation is impossible, for the inherent properties of a thing cannot be separated from it. The third formation remaineth and that is the voluntary one, that is, an unseen force described as the Ancient Power, causeth the elements to come together, every formation giving rise to a distinct being...Likewise every arrangement and formation that is not perfect in its order we designate as accidental, and that which is in its proper place and is the essential requisite of the other constituent parts, this we call a composition formed through will and knowledge. There is no doubt that these infinite beings and the association of these diverse elements arranged in countless forms must have proceeded from a Reality that could in no wise be bereft of will or un-

---

[90] *Flowers culled from the Rose Garden of Acca,* pp. 3–4 (These published recollections of words uttered by 'Abdu'l-Bahá during their pilgrimage, recorded by American believers.) Please see footnote #86 for an explanation of this source.

derstanding, and this infinite composition cast into infinite forms must have been caused by an all-embracing Wisdom. This none can dispute save he that is obstinate and stubborn, and denieth the clear and unmistakable evidence, and becometh the object of the blessed Verse: 'deaf, dumb, blind and shall return no more.'"[91]

SOURCE THREE

"It is a philosophical principle that the existence of phenomena implies composition, and that mortality or non-existence is equivalent to decomposition. For example, certain elements have come together and as a result of that composition man is here. Certain elements have entered into the structure of this flower. Certain organic or cellular elements have been utilized in the composition of every animal organism. Therefore, we can state that existence necessitates composition and death is another expression for decomposition. When there is disintegration amongst these composing elements, that is death. That is mortality. The elements, which have gone into the body of this flower and which have given existence to this form and shape, will finally disintegrate; this beautiful organism will decompose—and this we call mortality, death. Consequently the conclusion is that life means composition and death spells decomposition. On this account the materialists are of the opinion that life is the mere conjoining of elemental substances into myriad forms and shapes. The materialist comes to the conclusion that life in other words means composition; that wherever we find single elements combined

---

[91] SW XIV:4, 105, 108; reprinted in *Tablet to Dr. Forel*, pp. 16, 23. This is the only source of this proof which is entirely authenticated, inasmuch as it was written by 'Abdu'l-Bahá and translated by Shoghi Effendi. The other sources are from the utterances of 'Abdu'l-Bahá, translated into English by interpreters and recorded by pilgrims.

in aggregate form there we behold the phenomena of organic life. Now if life means composition of elements then the materialist may come to the conclusion of the non-necessity of a creator; for composition is all there is to it, and that is accomplished by adhesion or cohesion.

"In response to this we say that composition musts needs be of three kinds. This is a very important and subtle question. Give it your fullest attention. Then you will appreciate the point. One form of composition is termed philosophically the ACCIDENTAL form, another the VOLUNTARY, or a third, the INVOLUNTARY composition. As to the first or accidental composition: accidental composition, would signify that certain elements through inherent qualities and powers of attraction or affinity have been gathered together—have blended together and composed a certain form, being or organism. This can be proven to be false; for composition is an effect, and philosophically no effect is conceivable without causation. No effect can be conceived of without some primal cause. For example, this heat is an effect; but that energy which gives forth this phenomenon of heat is the cause. This light is an effect, but back of it is the energy which is the cause. Is it possible for this light to be separated from the energy whereof it is a property? That is impossible and inconceivable. It is self-evidently false. Accidental composition is, therefore, a false theory and may be excluded.

"As to the second form of composition—involuntary—this means that each element has within itself as an inherent property the power of composition. For example, the inherent quality of fire is burning or heat; heat is the property of fire. Humidity is the inherent nature or property of water. You cannot conceive of H20 which is the chemical form of water, without having humidity associated, for that is an inherent quality of water. The power of attraction has as its function attractive or magnetic qualities. We cannot separate attraction from that power. The power of repulsion has as its function repelling,— sending off. You cannot separate the effect from the cause. If these premises be true—and they are self-evident—then it would be impossible for a composite being, for certain elements which have gone into the make-up of a composite organism, to ever be decomposed, because the inherent nature of each element would be to hold fast together. As fire cannot be separated from heat, likewise the elemental being could not be subjected to decomposition, and this does not hold true, because we see decomposition everywhere. Hence this theory is untrue, inasmuch as we observe that after each composition there is a process of decomposition, which forever ends it.

"By this we learn that composition as regards phenomena is neither accidental nor involuntary. Then what have we left as a form of composition? It is the voluntary form of composition, which means that composition is effected through a superior will, that there is will expressed in this motive or action. It is thus proved that the existence of phenomena is effected through the eternal will, the will of the living, eternal and self-subsistent, and this is a rational proof concerning composition, wherefore there is no doubt or uncertainty."[92]

SOURCE FOUR – VERSION 1

"When we look upon all forms of phenomena we observe that they are the results of composition. For example, certain single atoms are brought together through the inherent law of elective affinity existing between these

---

[92] PUP 423–424, from an address by 'Abdu'l-Bahá, delivered on 10 November 1912 at 1700 Eighteenth Street, NW, Washington, D.C. (USA)

various particles, the result of which is the human being. A number of primordial atoms have gone into the
make-up of a plant, the result of which is in the flower.

"Again looking into the mineral kingdom we observe
that this law of cohesion is working in the same manner
in that kingdom, for we see that many atoms go into the
composition of a piece of stone which through purification may reach to the state of a mirror.

"In short, the existence of life depends upon the composition and decomposition of phenomena. When the
particles of a given composition are disintegrated this
may be called non-existence, but the original simple atoms will go back to their primary elements and are ever
existent.

"For instance, the body of man being the resultant factor
of the composition of these atoms, when this body becomes the subject of decomposition we call that death,
but those atoms of which the body was composed, being
simple and primordial, are indestructible. Consequently
it is proved that the existence of phenomena depends
upon composition and their mortality upon decomposition.

"This is a scientific principle; science approves of it, because it is not a matter of belief. There is a great difference between theories upheld by belief, and facts which
are substantiated by science.

"Beliefs are the susceptibilities of conscience, but scientific facts are the deductions of reason and inexorable
logic. Therefore it is logically proven that the existence
of phenomena depends upon composition, and their destruction upon disintegration.

Now going back to our subject and the facts upheld by
materialists. They state that inasmuch as it is proven

and upheld by science that the life of phenomena depends upon composition and their destruction upon disintegration, then where comes in the need or necessity of a Creator—the self-subsistent Lord?

"For we see with our own eyes that these infinite beings go through myriads of compositions and in every composition appearing under a certain form showing certain characteristic virtues, then we are independent of any divine maker. This is the argument of the materialists. On the other hand those who are informed of divine philosophy answer in the following terms:

"Composition is of THREE KINDS.

1. ACCIDENTAL composition.
2. INVOLUNTARY composition.
3. VOLUNTARY composition.

"There is no fourth kind of composition. Composition is restricted to these three categories.

"If we say that composition is accidental, this is philosophically a false theory, because then we have to believe in an effect without a cause, and philosophically no effect is conceivable without a cause. We cannot think of an effect without a primal cause, and composition being an effect, there must naturally be a cause behind it.

"As to the second composition, i.e., the involuntary composition. Involuntary composition means that each element has within it as an inherent function this power of composition. For example, certain elements have flowed towards each other, and as an inherent necessity of their being they are composed. That is, it is the immanent need of these elements to enter into composition.

"For example, the inherent quality of fire is burning or heat. Heat is an original property of fire.

"Humidity is the inherent nature of water. You cannot conceive of H_2O, which is the chemical form of water, without having humidity connected, for that is its inherent quality, inseparable and indivisible.

"Now as long as it is the inherent necessity of these elements to be composed, there should not be any decomposition. While we observe that after each composite organism, there is a process of decomposition we learn that the composition of the organisms of life is neither accidental nor involuntary. Then what have we as a form of composition? It is the third, that is the voluntary composition. And that means that the infinite forms of organisms are composed through a superior will, the eternal will, the will of the living and self-subsistent Lord. This is a rational proof, that the Will of the Creator is effected through the process of composition."[93]

SOURCE FOUR – VERSION 2

"Science teaches us that all forms of creation are the result of composition; for example, certain single atoms are brought together through the inherent law of affinity and the result is the human being. A number of primordial atoms have gone into the make-up of a plant, the result of which is this flower. Again, looking into the mineral kingdom, we observe that this law of attraction is working in the same manner. Many atoms go into the composition of a piece of stone which through purification may reach to the station of a mirror.

---

[93] SW VI:8, 62–64, address by 'Abdu'l-Bahá delivered Sunday, 9 February 1913, at 30 rue St. Didier, Paris (France)

"When the particles of a given composition are disintegrated, this may be called non-existence in that kingdom; but the original simple elements go back to their primary atoms and are ever existent. When the body of man becomes the subject of decomposition we call that death. That the existence of phenomena depends upon composition, and mortality upon decomposition, is a scientific fact and there is a great difference between facts sustained by science and theories upheld by blind belief which is the result of traditional susceptibility of conscience.

"The materialistic state that inasmuch as it is proved by science that the life of phenomena depends upon composition and its destruction upon disintegration, they question the necessity of a creator, the self-subsistent Lord. "For," argue the materialists, "we see with our own eyes that these infinite beings go through myriads of forms of composition and in every combination they bring about certain distinctive characteristics, so we are independent of any divine maker."

"Those informed with divine philosophy answer that there are three theories of composition: first, accidental composition; second, involuntary composition; third, voluntary composition.

"If we declare that construction is accidental, this is logically a false theory, because then we have to believe in an effect without a cause; our reason refuses to think of an effect without a primal cause.

"The second, involuntary composition, means that each element has within it an innate function of this power of composition—certain elements have flowed toward each other, their union being an inherent necessity of their being. But as long as we reason that it is the inherent necessity of those elements to enter into composition there should not be any necessity for decomposition; and inasmuch as we observe that there is a process of decomposition, we conclude that the constituent elements of life enter neither involuntarily nor accidentally, but voluntarily into composition—and this means that the infinite forms of organisms are composed through the superior will, the eternal will, the will of the living and self-subsistent Lord.

"This is a rational proof that the will of the Creator is effected through the process of composition. Ponder over this and strive to comprehend its significance, that you may be enabled to convey it to others; the more you think it over, the greater will be your degree of comprehension. Praise be to God that he has endowed you with a power through which you can penetrate mysteries. Verily, as you reflect deeply, ponder deliberately and think continually, the doors of knowledge will be opened unto you.

"I have been asked to speak of that which is eternal and that which is contingent. Is creation a manifestation or an emanation of God? There are two kinds of eternities. There is an eternity of essence, that which is without first cause, and an eternity of time, that which has no beginning. When you will understand these subjects all will become clear. Know of a certainty that every visible thing has a cause. For instance, this table is made by a carpenter; its originator is the carpenter.

"Therefore as such objects are not self created, they are not in the nature of things eternal; but need an auxiliary-transforming force, although in their essence they are very ancient in time; but their ancient and eternal existence is not due to the temporary form.

"For instance, the world of elements cannot be annihilated, because pure existence cannot be annihilated;

and what we observe are but transformative modifications in the composition of the essence. The combination of different elements has formed physical man; when the composition is destroyed the elements will return to their component parts. Complete annihilation cannot take place.

"The universe has never had a beginning. From the point of view of essence it transforms itself. God is eternal in essence and in time. He is his own existence and cause. This is why the material world is eternal in essence, for the power of God is eternal.

"A power is like a kingdom; it needs subjects and armies, for the constituents of a kingdom are rulers and subjects. The power of God is eternal and there have always been beings to manifest it; that is why we say that the worlds of God are infinite—there has never been a time when they did not exist. One can bring nothing forth from nothing, in the same way that which exists is never destroyed; the apparent annihilation is merely transmutation.

"A mineral compared to us may be said to be non-existent, but in its own sphere it lives. When we die our bodies return to the mineral and vegetable world. This example shows the inter-relationship of the different kingdoms which is erroneously called annihilation.

"All the wealth of contingencies is misery. If we know not the eternal, we are nothing, and as God is eternal, knowing God is a link to eternity. I pray you to reflect deeply upon this, that you may understand clearly. Many people think that creation is a manifestation of God, that the divine reality like unto the embryo in a seed, has come forth out of the seed and become a trunk, branches, leaves, flowers.

"The prophets teach differently. Creation is an emanation from the creator. It is impossible that the eternal should become limited. A tree never becomes a creature: it never acquires sight nor smell; yet both are creations of God—creations in emanation.

"Creation is like the sunlight; God is the sun. This light comes forth from the sun; that does not mean that the sun has become the light. The light emanates from the sun. Seek always to prove mysteries in the light of the rational mind. We must all become the light of this sun which is God; the light of the sun, the heat of the sun, the brilliancy of the sun, the bestowals of this sun.

"There is a point on which the philosophers and the prophets differ. The philosophers make education the test of knowledge, holding that any man who receives sufficient education can attain a state of perfection. That is to say man possesses the potentiality for every kind of progress and education enables him to bring this into the court of objectivity.

"The prophets say that something else is necessary. It is true that education transforms the desert into a rose garden, the virgin forest into an orchard, saplings into trees, and single flowers into double and treble flowers, but there is a fundamental difference in men. You may know ten children of one country, in the same school, under the same master, treated and fed in the same way. One of these children may make great progress, others may remain stationary. In the innate nature there are differences of memory, perception and intelligence. There is a superior, a middle and an inferior degree which corresponds to the difference in the fundamental estates of creation. While recognizing the influence of education we must also become acquainted with the innate disposition.

"The prophets are sent to educate this innate quality in humanity. They are like gardeners who sow the grain which afterward springs up in a thousand forms of advancement. The prophets are therefore the first educators of the world, the head masters of the world. However much man may advance in material civilization, if he remain ignorant of the spiritual civilization, his soul is still defaced.

"The prophets are sent to refresh the dead body of the world, to render the dumb, eloquent, to give peace to the troubled, to make illumined the indifferent and to set free from the material world all beings who are its captives. Leave a child to himself and he becomes ill-mannered and thoughtless. He must be shown the path, so that he may become acquainted with the world of the soul—the world of divine gifts.

"Existence is like a tree, and man is the fruit. If the fruit be sweet and agreeable, all is well, but if it be bitter it were far better there were none. Every man who has known the celestial bestowals is verily a treasury; if he remain ignorant of them, his non-existence were better than his existence. The tree which does not bring forth fruit is fit only for the fire. Strive night and day to change men into fruitful trees, virgin forests into divine orchards and deserts into rose gardens of significance. Light these lamps, that the dark world may become illumined...

"God in his wisdom has created all things. Nothing has been created without a special destiny, for every creature has an innate station of attainment. This flower has been created to mirror forth a harmonious ensemble of color and perfume. Each kingdom of nature holds potentialities and each must be cultivated in order to reach its fulfillment. The divine teachers desire man to be educated that he may attain to the high rank of his own reality, the deprivation of which is the rank of perdition. The flower needs light that it may achieve its fruitage; man needs the light of the Holy Spirit, and the measure of illumination throughout creation is proportionate to the different kingdoms.

"When we come to the estate of man, we find his kingdom is vested with a divine superiority. Compared to the animal, his perfection or his imperfection is superior. In comparison with man the perfection of a flower is insignificant. Yet if man remain content in an undeveloped state viewed from the point of capacity he is the lowest of creatures. If he attains unto his heritage through divine wisdom, then he becomes a clear mirror in which the beauty of God is reflected; he has eternal life and becomes a participator of the sun of truth. This is to show you how considerable are the degrees of human achievement.

"The aim of the prophet of God is to raise man to the degree of knowledge of his potentiality and to illumine him through the light of the kingdom, to transform ignorance into wisdom, injustice into justice, error into knowledge, cruelty into affection and incapability into progress. In short, to make all the attainments of existence resplendent in him.

"The greatest gift of man is universal love—that magnet which renders existence eternal. It attracts realities and diffuses life with infinite joy. If this love penetrate the heart of man, all the forces of the universe will be realized in him, for it is a divine power which transports him to a divine station and he will make no progress until he is illumined thereby. Strive to increase the love-power of reality, to make your hearts greater centers of attraction and to create new ideals and relationships.

"First of all, be ready to sacrifice your lives for one another, to prefer the general well-being to your personal well-being. Create relationships that nothing can shake; form an assembly that nothing can break up; have a mind that never ceases acquiring riches that nothing can destroy. If love did not exist, what of reality would remain? It is the fire of the love of God which renders man superior to the animal. Strengthen this superior force through which is attained all the progress in the world.

"May the light of divine advancement shine upon you. This is the glory and progress of man. This is eternal life.

"Brotherhood and sisterhood that is founded on a universal love is precious. It is not like the material kind which is soon forgotten and, perhaps, changed to hatred before this life is over. Material brothers and sisters seldom have lasting affection for each other, but this divine relationship is eternal. In the world of God it will become more clear and manifest."[94]

DISCUSSION OF THE PROOF OF VOLUNTARY COMPOSITION

'Abdu'l-Bahá at the outset asserts that there are three kinds of composition conceivable and only three kinds: accidental or by chance; necessary or involuntary or by force; and voluntary or by will. In pondering this subject we must first consider if there are not other possible kinds of composition conceivable. For example, is it possible that composition be magical, miraculous, without explanation? Can we admit that we simply don't know the origin of composition? In effect this seems to be the very solution to this question that has been adopted by many human cultures over the course of our planetary history, and to this day there are

---

[94] ABDP pp. 104–112; more complete version of the address by 'Abdu'l-Bahá delivered Sunday, 9 February 1913, at 30 rue St. Didier, Paris (France)

many human beings who regard life as essentially magical, miraculous and without explanation. This conviction has given rise in modern times to nihilism, which refuses to hold to any explanation or organization for human affairs and to existentialism which would have all human formulations regarded as personal and social fabrications bearing no necessary resemblance to actual reality and only of value to those individuals who subscribe to them. This intellectual relativism enjoys an extensive vogue especially among Westerners, and it may be compared with the views of some aboriginal animists, whom Westerners have so often called "primitive".

Nevertheless, 'Abdu'l-Bahá might address the modern relativist and the primordial animist, and ask if there were not some realities which are universally acknowledged among human beings, which may have different meanings for us which are personally conceived or socially constructed but which nevertheless we all perceive as real and existent. We will find that both parties will acknowledge that there are realities which we all affirm. What then is the source of those realities? If it is attested that the source of those realities is unknown, then it may be countered that what is unknown is only unknown as long as knowledge of that reality has not been acknowledged by an individual or a group of individuals. To be unknown does not of itself have a content, but rather it signifies an absence of content. The aboriginal animist may not know that all matter is made up of atoms (and their sub-particles). The modern relativist may not know that the family is the basic building block of all societies. The unknowing in either of these cases does not demonstrate the untruth of either of the propositions—these can be proven through the citation of evidence in a scientific manner which bellies personal conception (subjectivity) and social construction (socialization).

Everything that is known can be characterized as either accidental/chance, necessary/involuntary/compulsory or voluntary—this is the assertion of 'Abdu'l-Bahá. So we say, when someone falls off a ladder, stubs a toe, smashes a vehicle into a tree, or mixes salt into the pancake batter instead of sugar, that an accident has occurred. 'Abdu'l-Bahá uses other examples in a sequence — "it rained by chance, the sun cast its rays by chance; therefore vegetables grow". When we investigate each so-called accident further we find that while it appeared to be accidental, it appeared to be by chance, in fact it was caused by definite agents or factors. In effect, to speak of any occurrence as an accident is a turn of phrase, a form of speech and it is incorrect. It is a tenacious inheritance from the magical mindset of our ancestors, who did not know about causes, and it suits many of us just fine when we don't want to know what the causes of certain events are.

This is, in the modern age, an evasion of knowledge, and most often it also implies an evasion of responsibility—if we know we feel that we must act in accordance with that knowledge, and inasmuch as we don't want to feel obligated to do so, we prefer not to know, we say: "it was an accident." That someone who fell off the ladder did so because s/he didn't make sure that someone else was holding it firm when s/he began climbing. That someone who stubs a toe did not look ahead in the direction in which s/he was going or else the collision could have been avoided. The so-called traffic accident could be avoided by driving more carefully, more slowly, making sure the brakes were in good working order, and not driving after drinking alcohol or without adequate rest. The salt wouldn't have gone in the pancake mix if the cook had taken the precaution of tasting the white powder before spooning it in.

To cite 'Abdu'l-Bahá's examples—the rain does not fall by chance, it falls because certain conditions have come together under which it must fall; the sun does not shine by chance, it shines all the time and we feel it here on earth depending also on the fulfillment of certain precise conditions; and certainly vegetables do not grow by chance, but when there is enough watering and enough sunshine and enough nutrients from the ground and not too much wind. To one who has knowledge of why and how rain falls, sun shines and vegetables grow, it is clear and evident that there is no element of chance or accident operable in any of the three. To one who does not know it may seem that many things happen by chance, by accident. Inasmuch as science has discovered that for all phenomena there are causes, that nothing is accidental in the sense of being uncaused, we may put to side the objections of those who admit that they do not know (whether or not they will also admit that they are ignorant) in favor of the assertions of those who attest and prove that they do know. The principle argument against composition by accident or chance is the argument of cause, and this is examined more fully in the separate consideration of the rational proof for the existence of God, described as the Primal Cause.

The second variety of composition posited in this rational proof is described as forced/necessary/compulsory/involuntary. This appears to be a self-contradictory proof, inasmuch as examples of compositions having this attribute are described, including: 1)"for instance, fire attracts water, this is made through force—that is, the elements attract each other; when they come together they form an object"; 2)"the inherent property of fire is burning or heat; heat is a property of fire"; 3)"Humidity is the inherent nature or property of water"; 4)"The power of attraction has as its function attractive or magnetic qualities. We cannot separate attraction from that power"; 5)"The power of repulsion has as its function repelling,— sending off. You cannot separate the effect from the cause"; 6)"light that is the revealer of things"; 7)"heat that causeth the expansion of elements"; 8)" (solar) rays which are the essential property of the sun".

Let us consider first the examples of this phenomenon of forced/necessary/compulsory/involuntary attraction or composition:

1) Will scientists attest as to whether fire attracts water, and whether fire and water come together to form an object?

2) Is there a fire which does not have the inherent property of heat? According to the limited understanding of the author, such a fire does not exist.

3) Humidity is indeed a property of water, but what of frozen water—is it humid?

4) Magnetism attracts but not all phenomena, so, for example, metal will be attracted to a magnet while wood or glass will not be so attracted.

5) Repulsion will also occur through the approaching of two magnetically charged particles of the same nature, two positive charges or two negative charges, but again this is not universal but only pertaining to those magnetically charged particles and not to uncharged particles or to particles that are charged differently—one positive and one negative.

6) Light is only the revealer of things to those who are gifted with the faculty of sight (whether this is meant in the physical or the spiritual sense), but certainly for the seeing light reveals the appearances of things and cannot do otherwise.

7) Heat certainly causes the expansion of many elements, but whether this is universal is for the scientist to attest to.

8) The solar rays are here alleged to be inherent properties of the sun, and inasmuch as the sun is a ball of fire, and it has already been attested that heat (and we may add light) are inherent properties of fire, then we must assume that the solar rays are indeed inherent properties of the sun.

What do these examples actually signify? Surely they are not meant to serve as examples of phenomena which are always or universally forced, necessary, compulsory, involuntary. Rather do they serve to show how very few observable phenomena seem to demonstrate such a variety of composition. If we allow that all of the five examples cited are indeed indicative of involuntary composition, what do they show to be necessary prerequisites of such a state? If fire and water attract, if heat is inherent to fire and humidity to water and the magnetic powers of attraction and repulsion are integral and cannot be divided from their substances, then it is plain that as long as such a phenomenon exists, its inherent quality must exist. If there is no fire there need be no heat; if no water then no humidity; and likewise perhaps it could be affirmed that if there is not heat there is no fire and if no humidity then no water. Then, if this were to apply to composition, then it might be affirmed that if there is no cohesion or adhesion there is no composition, that cohesion or adhesion are the inherent properties of composition, and consequently that composition comes into being through adhesion or cohesion. What brings fire into existence? Fire has its causes. What brings water into existence? Water has its causes. What brings attraction and repulsion into existence? Both have their causes.

Hence the existence of fire, of water, of attraction and of repulsion, heat and light and even the solar ray is not an inherent quality of fire, water, attraction and repulsion. Existence is not an inherent quality of any composition, for if it were so then that composition could not cease to exist. Fire comes and goes, water comes and goes, so do attraction and repulsion, heat and light. At one time there were no solar rays and at some time in the distant future there will be no solar rays. Eternal existence is not an inherent attribute of any of these compositions. Is there any existence which has eternal duration? According to 'Abdu'l-Bahá,

> "the original simple atoms will go back to their primary elements and are ever existent...when this body becomes the subject of decomposition we call that death, but those atoms of which the body was composed, being simple and primordial, are indestructible."[95]

'Abdu'l-Bahá notes that if the world of existences were "formed through the power of attraction made by force...then there should not be the decomposition, because the elements attracted by the other must remain together everlastingly; corruption must not take place"; "for then the formation must be an inherent property of the constituent parts and the inherent property of a thing can in nowise be dissociated from it"; "then it would be impossible for a composite being, for certain elements which have gone into the make-up of a composite organism, to ever be decomposed, because the inherent nature of each element would be to hold fast

---

[95] SW VI:8, p. 63

together"; "as long as it is the inherent necessity of these elements to be composed, there should not be any decomposition." One argument against this assertion is that there are varying degrees of attraction and cohesion and hence of composition, that hydrogen and oxygen are attracted under certain circumstances to form H_2O, and that under other circumstances—namely heat of 100 °C or 212 °F (or higher)—these elements separate again. What seems to be a permanent attraction proves under different circumstances to be an arrangement of convenience! This is rather a proof of the unacceptability of involuntary composition than one in favor of such a notion.

A clear delineation must be made between attraction, bonding on the one hand, and inherent qualities on the other. No combination of atoms or elements is eternal, inherent to the existence of any of those atoms or elements. Such compositions come and go. If composition was an inherent quality of a composite being then they would remain forever. The duration of composite beings is of course extremely varied, with certain rocks remaining for millions of years, certain trees for hundreds of years, while animals may live between a century and a few hours. This life is the duration of their composition, and decomposition usually begins shortly upon the composition coming to maturity (or, in the case of the rock, immediately after it comes into existence).

There is but one remaining variety of formation which remains for 'Abdu'l-Bahá. We have tried to imagine other varieties but to no avail. To cite another formula, that depicting human character, which is described as composed of three elements, the innate, the inherited and the acquired, there may be some who will assert that there may be other elements of human character besides the innate, the inherited and the acquired, and they may posit extraterrestrial influence such as UFOs, angels, devils, spirits of the human deceased, spirits of magical animals or plants, fairies, devas, and of course the sun, the planets and the stars. While there may indeed be extraterrestrial (or metaphysical) influences upon human characters, the description still stands that they are composed of three kinds of elements: innate, that is, endowed to the soul at conception; inherited, that is, endowed to the body at conception; and acquired, that is, learned or otherwise absorbed during the lifespan—this certainly allows for the existence of extraterrestrial influences, although confining them to the lifespan and disallowing them for a posited pre-existence.

It may be claimed that this kind of argument amounts to reductionism, that the forms of existence are too complicated and too various to be able to conveniently explain. This retreat from reality which the relativist carefully cultivates so as to be free to interpret his/her world in whatever way s/he pleases, this hiding behind details, behind the veil of knowledge, obfuscates the cogency of this rational proof. Two forms of composition have been eliminated from consideration. A third was tentatively introduced, in order that certain partisans thereof might not cry too much at being left out of the discussion. What remains, what the argument has reduced itself to is the consideration of the third and final possible mode of composition. This third way asserts "that all objects in the world are made or formed by will"; "an unseen force described as the Ancient Power, causeth the elements to come together, every formation giving rise to a distinct being...There is no doubt that these infinite beings and the association of these diverse elements arranged in countless forms must have proceeded from a Reality that could in no wise be bereft of will or understanding"; "composition is effected through a superior will, that there is will expressed in this motive or action"; "the infinite forms of organisms are composed through a superior will, the eternal will, the will of the living and self-subsistent Lord."

Many of you readers may wonder how we came from considering such apparently scientific and philosophical matters as inherent qualities and accidental formation to such a straightforward assertion not only of the existence of God but of God as creator of all existence and as creator through the instrumentality of will. How have we come so far and so deep into theological territory?

First of all, if the formation of composition can be known—and divine philosophy asserts that it is known—and if we have rejected the previously described categories of accidental and involuntary composition then the third variety is causal. Composition is not accidental, for then it would have no cause, nor is it inherent for then it would be inherent and could not be changed, but as composition leads to decomposition then it must always be preceded by a cause, and a cause is preceded by a cause and finally there must be a First Cause.

This First Cause is identified by 'Abdu'l-Bahá as God. But as God is the First Cause, then He is separated from His own causal act of bringing causes into existence, and this first act is called will.

> "The first thing to emanate from God is that universal reality which the ancient philosophers termed the 'First Intellect' and which the people of Bahá call the 'Primal Will'."[96]

Furthermore, it is explained that the First Cause did not set the chain of causes in motion by accident or out of necessity but rather voluntarily, through an act of will. What scientific evidence is there in support of the existence of a Primal Will? First of all, let us consider the life-forms in the midst of which we exist. Birds make nests, ants make hills, bees make hives, beavers build dams, and various other animals create their own homes. Whether they create their homes through an act of will or through an inherited instinct we do not know for sure, but it seems most likely that this is through instinct.

Human beings, on the other hand, not only make their homes but roads and trains and telephones and paintings and symphony orchestras and literally millions of creations and all are agreed that we do so through acts of will, not through instinct. We create not accidentally, nor because of an inherent property of our nature but because we choose to do so. When we choose not to cre-

---

[96] SAQ IV:53.5

ate we are capable of sitting on the wayside of life and watching, simply watching, simply living. Inasmuch as the universe about us has not come into existence accidentally, nor because of any inherent properties requiring it to do so, then it must have come into being through an act of will. As we are creators so God our creator must be a creator, and indeed God is the most perfect of creators! This is an example of inductive rather than deductive reasoning which may account for some of the resistance and opposition to such an affirmation. But later we will encounter a deductive proof for the existence of creation, which will assert that God is the only necessary and self-sufficient and independent existence and God has always been a Creator and hence Creation has always existed and will always exist, but without God there would be no creation. This is the science of reality speaking, and it speaks with authority, and in ways that we are not used to hearing and understanding.

The superior will of the Ancient Power is then manifest in all of the creations of God, and "the innate nature bestowed by God upon man is purely good"[97]; "The innate capacity, which is the creation of God, is wholly and entirely good—in the innate nature there is no evil"[98]; "In the innate nature of things there is no evil—all is good."[99] This is an astonishing teaching for those who have been reared in the dualism of both the East and the West, the North and the South, for a belief in the essential existence of evil is widespread throughout almost all human populations. This, 'Abdu'l-Bahá asserts, is in agreement with the rational proof for the existence of God, for if there is one reality,[100] there must also be one Primal Cause, one Primal Will, that must be either good or evil or both, and as evil is the absence of good and not an independent existence then the original God is good. Evil is

---

[97] SAQ IV:57.3,
[98] SAQ IV:56.9
[99] SAQ IV:56.10
[100] PUP 127, 175, 222

godlessness, absence of godliness. Chapters Four through Six will treat this subject in detail.

'Abdu'l-Bahá introduced this proof as one of those "which establish scientifically the existence of God."[101] Likewise, it is introduced by the following statement: "This is a scientific principle; science approves of it, because it is not a matter of belief. There is a great difference between theories upheld by belief, and facts which are substantiated by science. Beliefs are the susceptibilities of conscience, but scientific facts are the deductions of reason and inexorable logic."[102] This is an important statement, inasmuch as it establishes beyond doubt the authority of divine philosophy; divine philosophy takes its place as one of the sciences, indeed as the spiritual contingent of science in its entirety, as the repository of the science of reality which is revealed by the prophets. In establishing the existence of God, it is proving that existence by means of "facts which are substantiated by science", "scientific facts...the deductions of reason and inexorable logic". Many readers have difficulty understanding scientific facts and arguments. It is to be expected that this scientific proof will fall upon deaf ears. But nonetheless 'Abdu'l-Bahá does not mince words—these are facts which substantiate the existence of God, not "theories upheld by belief". There are many proofs and evidences for the existence of God, and this is not surprising considering that divine philosophy establishes the fact, the scientifically substantiated fact of the existence of God.

SECOND PROOF: MAN DID NOT CREATE HIMSELF

"Among the proofs and arguments for the existence of God is the fact that man has not created himself, but rather that his creator and fashioner is another than he."[103]

---

[101] SW VI:8, 62
[102] SW VI:8, 62–63
[103] SAQ I:2.1

There are those among my readers who find attractive and even the compelling the notion that the individual human being creates himself, chooses his/her own body and personality and life-plan. However, even these ones, and there are not many who entertain such notions, do not know from whence came man, the species. The so-called Darwinian theory of evolution is much more popular, and according to the most prevalent understanding of this theory, man did not properly speaking have a creator and designer—man simply evolved through the natural process of the survival of the fittest. While such a process does not of itself posit a creator/designer, neither does it indicate how the creation and design of man was evolved, what caused man to evolve as s/he did.

Is the creator and designer of man, man? While the creator in the sense of parent of one man is the union of a man and a woman, and hence in this sense the creator of man is man (and woman), and while the parent/s of that man to a large extent design the offspring, first of all by virtue of genetic hereditary endowment, secondly in the womb of the mother, thirdly in the home and surrounding environment, notwithstanding this creative and designing influence upon each man by his/her parent/s, inasmuch as human beings have not always existed there must have been primal parents and these must have been created and designed by something or someone other than themselves.

All mythologies seek to explain the first appearance of man. Virtually all of them have man issuing from a single primal parent and that parent is identified as a deity. Why do we humans believe that we are not self-created, and that we have not simply evolved from primordial sludge? Is it not possible that we believe so because it is so? However, this is not a scientific argument. The scientific argument states that man has an original antecedent, and whether that ancestor was ape-like (and man is a hybrid or mutant from a vanished race of apes) or divine, it is not possible that man is without a source. This is then a causal argument, but one with a special twist, inasmuch as we are the subject and man is indeed a self-centered being. Where do I come from? My mother's womb? The joining of my mother's egg and my father's sperm? Yes, that accounts for part of me. Likewise, my rearing, my upbringing and my education under the aegis of my parents' accounts for much of me. But that is not all. In fact, what is most important, most essential about any person is that which cannot be derived from inheritance or education—Johann Sebastian Bach did not inherit his genius for composition from his parents, nor did he learn to be a genius from his upbringing. His inheritance and his education prepared him to channel his genius in a particular direction perhaps, but the phenomenal creativity of that individual man is in no way attributable to either of those parental influences. From whence did it issue? Was it accidental? No, it must have a cause or causes. Was it involuntary? No, for this genius was not inherent to all children of that couple. Was it voluntary? Yes, but not merely voluntary in being chosen and willed by that gifted individual himself, for many individuals who wish to be gifted are not and many who are gifted do not wish to be; the voluntariness of J. S. Bach's genius (or creativity to employ a less value-laden word) was also chosen for him. That choice points to the existence of God, even as the ultimate creation and design of man requires the existence of God.

THIRD PROOF: MAN CANNOT CREATE ANOTHER BEING

"And it is certain and indisputable that the creator of man is not like man himself, because a powerless being cannot create another being, and an active creator must possess all perfections to produce his handiwork."[104]

Now in what sense is man powerless? Man is quite used to thinking of himself (especially, I might stress, "him"-self) as powerful. Indeed, 'Abdu'l-Bahá affirms the same in this passage:

---

[104] SAQ I:2.1

"The sun, that colossal center of our solar system, the giant stars and planets, the towering mountains, the earth itself and its kingdoms of life lower than the human—all are captives of nature except man. No other created thing can deviate in the slightest degree from obedience to natural law. The sun in its glory and greatness millions of miles away is held prisoner in its orbit of universal revolution, captive of universal natural control. Man is the ruler of nature. According to natural law and limitation he should remain upon the earth, but behold how he violates this command and soars above the mountains in airplanes. He sails in ships upon the surface of the ocean and dives into its depths in submarines. Man makes nature his servant; he harnesses the mighty energy of electricity, for instance, and imprisons it in a small lamp for his uses and convenience. He speaks from the East to the West through a wire. He is able to store and preserve his voice in a phonograph. Though he is a dweller upon earth, he penetrates the mysteries of starry worlds inconceivably distant. He discovers latent realities within the bosom of the earth, uncovers treasures, penetrates secrets and mysteries of the phenomenal world and brings to light that which according to nature's jealous laws should remain hidden, unknown and unfathomable. Through an ideal inner POWER man brings these realities forth from the invisible plane to the visible. This is contrary to nature's law."[105]

While man does not have great physical power in comparison with certain other animals—oxen, elephants, horses, lions among others—and while he is physically like an insect in comparison with the enormous resources of tidal power, volcanic power and hurricane power, man has discovered and learned to control a source of energy which is as destructive and potentially

---

[105] PUP 177–178

also as creative as any force of nature known on this planet—nuclear fission. How then is man powerless? Man is powerless to create out of nothing. Man is powerless to create another being. Man can modify other beings, through genetic engineering, through breeding, hybridization, and man can even create alloys of metals and plastics by combining various materials which already exist into new materials which have never existed before. However, man cannot create from nothing, and hence man is powerless in comparison with the First Cause which has created from nothing. Does man possess all perfections? It is evident that there are many perfections which man does not possess—this is not necessary to demonstrate with examples and arguments. But why is it stated that "an active creator must possess all perfections to produce his handiwork"? This seems to be an argument from design, that is, an argument that the Creator of man must possess all perfections in order the He be able to create man because man is such an exemplary creature. We will encounter this design argument later in more detail. Also, it may be understood as an argument for a Creator possessing all perfections, all attributes in the superlative for otherwise He would be unable to create; for creation is beyond the capacity of man, and man has many perfections and therefore his Creator must be far more perfect than His creation.

FOURTH PROOF: PERFECT CREATION
REQUIRES PERFECT CREATOR

"Is it possible for the handiwork to be perfect and the craftsman imperfect? Is it possible for a painting to be a masterpiece and the painter to be deficient in his craft, notwithstanding that he is its creator?"[106]

Both of these statements are most challenging, inasmuch as they follow a clear statement of the powerlessness of the creation

---

[106] SAQ I:2.2

(in this case: man), and the inability of man due to that power-lessness to create another being.

Certainly powerlessness cannot be regarded as a perfection, and therefore we ask, 'How can the creation be considered perfect?' From this point of view then the powerlessness of the creature is not an imperfection, indeed it is a mark, a sign of the creature's perfection—for the creature's powerlessness makes him dependent upon the Creator and this is the perfect design of the Creator at work. Man has been declared unable to create another being, and the subsequent reference to the painter and his painting, as well as the following phrase which makes "art" and "creation" equivalents, seems to contradict such a statement, inasmuch as the painter referred to is most likely to be human. The example is true however because a painting is not another being, and while art and creation are equivalents, they are not absolutely the same. The argument being made in any case is not in conflict with the Third Proof—it is that the perfection of the creation demonstrates the perfection of the creator even as the masterpiece painting demonstrates the master painter.

> "For instance, we observe that the existence of beings is conditioned upon the coming together of various elements and their non-existence upon the decomposition of their constituent elements. Thus, as we observe the coming together or elements giving rise to the existence of beings, and knowing that beings are infinite, they being the effect, how can the Cause be finite?"[107]

This is not only another statement of this Fourth Proof, but also a statement of two other proofs, one being that of voluntary composition —for if composition were accidental then there would be no attribution to its Cause, and if it were necessary then decomposition would be impossible— and the other being that of the First Cause. 'Abdu'l-Bahá thus states three distinct proofs in the frame of one statement, which is a feat worthy of the esteem

---

[107] SW XIV:4, 105; reprinted in *Tablet to Dr. Forel*, p. 16.

of even the most skeptical reader. Logically it is asserted that the Cause must be greater than the effect, and inasmuch as the effects are infinite, the Cause must be infinite.

FIFTH PROOF: PERFECT CREATOR SUPERIOR TO PERFECT CREATION

> "The painting cannot be like the painter, for otherwise it would have painted itself. And no matter how perfect the painting may be, in comparison with the painter it is utterly deficient."[108]

This seems to be a continuation of the Third Proof, but it introduces two new elements so it is being treated separately—the fundamental difference between the created and the creator; and no matter how perfect the creation is, in comparison with its creator it is in comparison without perfections.

First of all, those who claim that man created himself—are there any of those remaining?—will cease upon this point to state that man is like his creator and therefore he is his own creator. However, anyone who knows the difference between a painting and a painter will understand that a painting is incapable of painting itself—it has no imagination, no instruments, no bodily limbs, no consciousness, in fact no existence apart from the existence given to it by the painter. This is exactly the difference between the Creator and His creation—in comparison with Him the creation has no consciousness, no power, no existence because the creation is totally dependent upon its Creator for everything that it is. The Báb has expressed this truth cogently: "All are His servants, and all abide by His bidding." Furthermore, the attributes and existence of the painting are insignificant in comparison with the far superior attributes and existence of the painter; likewise, the perfection of the creation proves the incomparably greater perfection of the Creator.

---

[108] SAQ I:2.2

SIXTH PROOF: IMPERFECTIONS OF CREATION
PROOF OF PERFECTIONS OF GOD

"The very deficiencies of the contingent world testify to God's perfections. For example, when you consider man, you observe that he is weak, and this very weakness of the creature betokens the power of One Who is Eternal and Almighty; for were it not for power, weakness could not be imagined. Thus the weakness of the creature is evidence of the power of God: Without power there could be no weakness. This weakness makes it evident that there is a power in the world. Again, in the contingent world there is poverty; hence there must be wealth for there to be poverty in the world. In the contingent world there is ignorance; hence there must be knowledge for there to be ignorance. If there were no knowledge, neither could there be ignorance; for ignorance is the non-existence of knowledge, and if there were no existence, non-existence could not be. It is certain that the entire contingent world is subject to an order and a law which it can never disobey. Even man is forced to submit to death, sleep, and other conditions—that is, in certain matters he is compelled, and this very compulsion implies the existence of One Who is All-Compelling. So long as the contingent world is characterized by dependency, and so long as this dependency is one of its essential requirements, there must be One Who in His own Essence is independent of all things. In the same way, the very existence of a sick person shows that there must be one who is healthy; for without the latter the existence of the former could not be established. It is therefore evident that there is an Eternal and Almighty One Who is the sum of all perfections, for otherwise He would be even as the creatures. Likewise, throughout the world of existence the smallest created thing attests to the existence of a creator. For instance, this piece of bread attests that it has a maker."[109]

This proof is based upon a maxim which reads as follows: "we know things philosophically by their antitheses."[110] Before proceeding with a consideration of any of these antithesis examples, let us first review the other examples of antitheses cited in divine philosophy.

"Furthermore, it is quite evident that our kind of life, our form of existence, is limited and that the reality of all accidental phenomena is, likewise, limited. The very fact that the reality of phenomena is limited well indicates that there must needs be an unlimited reality, for were there no unlimited, or infinite, reality in life, the finite being of objects would be inconceivable. To make it plainer for you, if there were no wealth in the world, you would not have poverty. If there were no light in the world, you could not conceive of darkness… We know, for example, that poverty is the lack of wealth. Where there is no knowledge, there is ignorance. What is ignorance? It is the absence of knowledge. Therefore, our limited existence is a conclusive proof that there is an unlimited reality, and this is a shining proof and an evident argument."[111] "And further, all created things are limited, and this very limitation of all beings proveth the reality of the Limitless; for the existence of a limited being denoteth the existence of a Limitless One."[112] "Now as to the Power that knoweth no limitations; limitation itself proveth the existence of the unlimited, for the limited is known through the unlimited, just as weakness proveth the existence of wealth. Without wealth there would be

---

[109] SAQ I:2.3–6
[110] PUP 425
[111] PUP 424–425
[112] SWAB 51

> no poverty, without knowledge no ignorance, without light no darkness. Darkness itself is a proof of the existence of light for darkness is the absence of light."[113]

The maxim or law of knowing through antitheses is much encountered in divine philosophy. It is known in the East as the law of yin/yang, of Shiva/Shakti, of lingam/yoni, of positive/negative—of dualities, opposites. In the West, and hence in Jewish, Christian and Islamic literature this argument from opposites was first articulated by Plato.[114] In philosophy it is understood that the absence of any quality cannot be imagined or conceived of if that quality is not imagined or conceived of. Hunger is recognized because we are familiar with satiation, and likewise thirst is experienced because we also know the feeling of adequate fluidity. Likewise it is true that one who has experienced hunger or thirst truly appreciates and understands satiation and fluidity.

This proof, along with all others, addresses itself to the human condition and to the human experience and consciousness. All human beings experience limitations, poverty, darkness, sickness, weakness, ignorance, dependency and imperfections, and the human condition is such that all must experience these imperfections because we live in the contingent world and everything in this world is limited. Every

> "man is forced to submit to death, sleep, and other conditions—that is, in certain matters he is compelled, and this very compulsion implies the existence of One Who is All-Compelling. So long as the contingent world is characterized by dependency, and so long as this dependency is one of its essential requirements, there must be One Who in His own Essence is independent of all things.".[115]

---

[113] SW XIV:4, 106

[114] Republic (II, 381c), also found in Aristotle (Frag. 16 R³); given its first explicit formulation as the "fourth way" of Aquinas (proof 4).

[115] SAQ I:2.5

The very existence of religion is testimony to the human rec-ognition of the antitheses of what each individual experiences — the unlimited, wealth, light, health, strength, knowledge, inde-pendence, perfection—and the understanding that those antith-eses are related to an ultimate, a primordial zenith. In fact, the closest that man can come to experience of that ultimate in reali-ty, which is the experience of that ultimate in himself, that expe-rience is one of transcending the contingent consciousness and partaking of the eternal consciousness. The Buddha Gautama lived as a prince, experiencing wealth, light, health, strength, in-dependence, perfection and freedom from limitations to a super-lative degree associated with his station and condition, and one day he observed the poverty, darkness, sickness, weakness, igno-rance, dependency, imperfections and the myriad limitations of some of his subjects, and from this he learned that all contingent existence is limited, that his princely experience of life was un-true not because it was confined to a tiny elite rather than shared by all men but rather because the most princely life is still limited and imperfect in comparison with the life of the Unlimited and Perfect.

SEVENTH PROOF: THE COMPELLED IMPLIES
THE EXISTENCE OF THE ALL-COMPELLING

"It is certain that the entire contingent world is subject to an order and a law which it can never disobey. Even man is forced to submit to death, sleep, and other con-ditions—that is, in certain matters he is compelled, and this very compulsion implies the existence of One Who is All-Compelling."[116]

At first reading this seems to be an argument by antithesis, a version of the Sixth Proof; however, a true antithesis would state that because we know of the existence of one who is com-

---

[116] SAQ I:2.5

pelled then we must also recognize the existence of one who is independent of all rules and subject to no laws. A governor is not however one who is independent of all compulsion; One Who is All-Compelling has power over others, and can compel their obedience. Another formulation of this argument would be to state that as there are subjects or slaves to rule there must also be rulers and masters. Subjects without rulers and slaves without masters are freedmen, and freedmen are not compelled. This is precisely the appeal of anarchy for the aspiring hedonist or libertine. If s/he seeks a state of being that is without constraints then it must be without One Who is All-Compelling. This is impossible, for as long as man exists in this contingent world he is compelled to adhere to certain requirements regardless of his dreams, his aspirations or even his will; for every man must sleep, every man must eat and drink, every man must breathe, every man must die.

This proof is arrived at by deduction, for 'Abdu'l-Bahá perceives the compelling factors that constrain the freedom and limit the independence of man and other creatures, and sees that no reality that man has experienced is uncompelled; he thereby comes to the conclusion that there must be One Who is All-Compelling. Constraints do not come into existence spontaneously. In human experience—and this is the only experience that human beings can have—natural laws are caused even as human laws are caused, and this chain of causation leads eventually to One Who is All-Compelling. Many of the prophets have called God the King of the worlds.

EIGHTH PROOF: COORDINATOR FOR UNIVERSE REQUIRED

> "It is obvious that all created things are connected one to another by a linkage complete and perfect, even, for example, as are the members of the human body. Note how all the members and component parts

of the human body are connected one to another. In the same way, all the members of this endless universe are linked one to another. The foot and the step, for example, are connected to the ear and the eye; the eye must look ahead before the step is taken. The ear must hear before the eye will carefully observe. And whatever member of the human body is deficient, produceth a deficiency in the other members. The brain is connected with the heart and stomach, the lungs are connected with all the members. So it is with the other members of the body.

"And each one of these members hath its own special function. The mind force—whether we call it pre-existent or contingent—doth direct and co-ordinate all the members of the human body, seeing to it that each part or member duly performeth its own special function. If, however, there be some interruption in the power of the mind, all the members will fail to carry out their essential functions, deficiencies will appear in the body and the functioning of its members, and the power will prove ineffective.

"Likewise, look into this endless universe: a universal power inevitably existeth, which encompasseth all, directing and regulating all the parts of this infinite creation; and were it not for this Director, this Co-ordinator, the universe would be flawed and deficient. It would be even as a madman; whereas ye can see that this endless creation carrieth out its functions in perfect order, every separate part of it performing its own task with complete reliability, nor is there any flaw to be found in all its workings. Thus it is clear that a Universal Power existeth, directing and regulating this infinite universe. Every rational mind can grasp this fact."[117]

---

[117] SWAB 47–48

"By nature is meant those inherent properties and necessary relations derived from the realities of things. And these realities of things, though in the utmost diversity, are yet intimately connected one with the other. For these diverse realities an all-unifying agency is needed that shall link them all one to the other. For instance, the various organs and members, the parts and elements, that constitute the body of man, though at variance, are yet all connected one with the other by that all-unifying agency known as the human soul, that causeth them to function in perfect harmony and with absolute regularity, thus making the continuation of life possible. The human body, however, is utterly unconscious of that all-unifying agency, and yet acteth with regularity and dischargeth its functions according to its will..."[118]

"Now concerning nature, it is but the essential properties and the necessary relations inherent in the realities of things. And though these infinite realities are diverse in their character yet they are in the utmost harmony and closely connected together. As one's vision is broadened and the matter observed carefully, it will be made certain that every reality is but an essential requisite of other realities. Thus to connect and harmonize these diverse and infinite realities an All-unifying Power is necessary, that every part of existent being may in perfect order discharge it own function.

"Consider the body of man, and let the part be an indication of the whole. Consider how these diverse parts and members of the human body are closely connected and harmoniously united one with the other. Every part is the essential requisite of all other parts and has

---

[118] SW XIV:4, p. 104; reprinted in *Tablet to Dr. Forel*, p. 13

a function by itself. It is the mind that is the all-unifying agency that so uniteth all the component parts one with the other that teach dischargeth its special function in perfect order, and thereby cooperation and reaction are made possible. All parts function under certain laws that are essential to existence. Should that all-unifying agency that directeth all these parts to be harmed in any way there is no doubt that the constituent parts and members will cease functioning properly; and though that all-unifying agency in the temple of man be not sensed or seen and the reality thereof be unknown, yet by its effects it manifesteth itself with the greatest power.

"Thus it hath been proven and made evident that these infinite beings in this wondrous universe will discharge their functions properly only when directed and controlled by that Universal Reality, so that order may be established in the world. For example, interaction and cooperation between the constituent parts of the human body are evident and indisputable, yet this does not suffice; an all-unifying agency is necessary that shall direct and control the component parts, so that these through interaction and cooperation may discharge in perfect order their necessary and respective functions.

"You are well aware, praise be the Lord, that both interaction and cooperation are evident and proven amongst all beings, whether large or small. In the case of large bodies interaction is as manifest as the sun, whilst in the case of small bodies, though interaction be unknown, yet the part is an indication of the whole. All these interactions therefore are connected with that all-embracing power which is their pivot, their center, their source and their motive power.

"For instance, as we have observed, cooperation among the constituent parts of the human body is clearly established, and these parts and members render services unto all the component parts of the body. For instance, the hand, the foot, the eye, the ear, the mind, the imagination all help the various parts and members of the human body, but all these interactions are linked by an unseen, all-embracing power, that causeth perfect regularity. This is the inner faculty of man, that is his spirit and his mind, both of which are invisible.

"In like manner consider machinery and workshops and the interaction existing among the various component parts and sections, and how connected they are one with the other. All these relations and interactions, however, are connected with a central power which is their motive force, their pivot and their source. This central power is either the power of steam or the skill of the master-mind.

"It hath therefore been made evident and proved that interaction, cooperation and inter-relation amongst beings are under the direction and will of a motive Power which is the origin, the motive force and the pivot of all interactions in the universe."[119]

This proof is described in such detail and in such a logical and scientific fashion that 'Abdu'l-Bahá regards it not only as reasonable but "fact". This is an important distinction, to assert that

"it is clear that a Universal Power existeth, directing and regulating this infinite universe. Every rational mind can grasp this FACT."[120]

---

[119] SW XIV:106–107; reprinted in *Tablet to Dr. Forel*, pp. 20–21
[120] SWAB 49

In a statement of the First Proof, with which the reader is already familiar, 'Abdu'l-Bahá affirms:

> "There is a great difference between theories upheld by belief, and facts which are substantiated by science. Beliefs are the susceptibilities of conscience, but scientific facts are the deductions of reason and inexorable logic."[121]

How can a metaphysical affirmation be regarded as "fact"? It can be so if the affirmation is based upon other "facts" to which no objection or divergency can be demonstrated.

This argument has various facets:

1) The perfect functioning of the universe requires a co-ordinator, an all-unifying agency;

2) The perfect functioning of the human body requires a co-ordinator, an all-unifying agency—this is found in the mind, the soul; this is an example of the requirement for such an agency in the universe: "the part is an indication of the whole."[122]

3) Interaction and cooperation and inter-relation between all things, large or small requires an "all-embracing power which is their pivot, their center, their source and their motive power."[123]

4) Interaction and connection among various component parts of machinery and workshops (factories?) is effected through "a central power which is their motive force, their pivot and their source."[124]

5) Without "this Director, this Co-ordinator, the universe would be flawed and deficient. It would be even as a madman..."[125]

This argument is clearly derived from observation, logical and scientific in spirit, of the universe; of a great many phenomena, large and small; of the human body in particular; of machin-

---

[121] SW VI:8, 63
[122] SW XIV:4, 106; reprint in *Tablet to Dr. Forel*, p. 21
[123] SW XIV:4, 107; reprint in *Tablet to Dr. Forel*, p. 22
[124] Ibid., p. 23
[125] SWAB 48

ery and factories. The argument is inductive, inasmuch as it derives a generality from the study of particular instances, in this case from observations of many of the interactions, connections, inter-relations among phenomena in the universe that there are such interactions, connections and inter-relations among all phenomena in the universe. It is also inductive in stating that "the part is an indication of the whole" in the case of the universe. It is well known that the genetic identity of every cell of the human body is identical and in this sense then, regardless of the difference in function and composition of the various parts of the body, the body is a whole, the body is one organism. This is the case of the genetic identity of other organisms, of plants and of animals. The part, any part of any particular organism is an indication of the whole of that organism by virtue of its genetic identity being stamped as it were upon every cell of that organism. So also 'Abdu'l-Bahá asserts that the fundamental identity of each existence in the universe is indicative of the existence of the whole.

This assertion however is not established upon belief, upon opinion, but rather upon fact. The fact which ties together all existences in the universe is this:

> "the original simple atoms will go back to their primary elements and are ever existent...those atoms of which the body was composed, being simple and primordial, are indestructible."[126]

While this is a fact that is evident to all scientists and therefore the reader may be acquainted therewith, there is another fact which 'Abdu'l-Bahá proves to be as compelling a proof of the connection between all existences as the evidence from the structure of matter, and this is the reality of the spirit.

> "The spirit however possesseth various grades and stations. As to the existence of spirit in the mineral: it is

---

[126] SW VI:8, 63

indubitable that minerals are endowed with a spirit and life according to the requirements of that stage. This unknown secret, too, hath become known unto the materialists who now maintain that all beings are endowed with life, even as He saith in the Qur'an, 'All things are living.' In the vegetable world too, there is the power of growth, and that power of growth is the spirit. In the animal world there is the sense of feeling, but in the human world there is an all-embracing power. In all the preceding stages the power of reason is absent, but the soul existeth and revealeth itself The sense of feeling understandeth not the soul, whereas the reasoning power of the mind proveth the existence thereof. In like manner the mind proveth the existence of an unseen Reality that embraceth all beings, and that existeth and revealeth itself in all stages, the essence whereof is beyond the grasp of the mind."[127]

Hence, 'Abdu'l-Bahá asserts that life, that spirit, that what we may think of as energy characterizes all existences in the universe, and this also links them all together. Not only are all existences coordinated by an all-unifying agency, but that agency reveals itself in stages in all of those existences, and while

"the mineral world understandeth neither the nature nor the perfections of the vegetable world; the vegetable world understandeth not the nature of the animal world, neither the animal world the nature of the reality of man..."[128] "...but in the human world there is an all-embracing power...the reasoning power of the mind...that discovereth and embraceth all things."[129]

These existences which reveal the spirit, the life of God in stages do not understand that spirit, do not recognize God, but

---

[127] SW XIV:4, 102–103; reprinted in *Tablet to Dr. Forel*, pp. 9–10
[128] Ibid.
[129] Ibid.

man, because of "the reasoning power of the mind" understands "the existence of an unseen Reality that embraceth all beings..."[130]

While the materialist, the agnostic and the atheist may assert that God is defined according to human experience, that God is therefore in the image of man rather than the converse, 'Abdu'l-Bahá does not disdain to cite the functioning of the human body in relationship to the mind as evidence of the function of the universe under the all-unifying agency of God.

Nor are the creations of man excluded from the argument—machinery and workshops (factories?) are cited as examples of phenomena which are "connected with a central power which is their motive force, their pivot and their source."[131] Every machine has a central power which is its motive force, pivot and source, whether it be a computer chip or electric generator or atomic reactor of internal combustion chamber; in another sense, every machine has another sort of central power, whether it be its human operator or a computer; finally, every machine has its original central power which is the man who invented and built it. Why is 'Abdu'l-Bahá citing examples which could be identified with the denials of the materialist agnostic or atheist? Because of the principle that "the part is an indication of the whole". This argument is so convincing that every existence in the universe can be shown to demonstrate that the co-ordination and inter-relation of parts requires a Coordinator. A universe, or indeed any existence within a universe without such a Coordinator "would be even as a madman",[132] lacking harmony and order and perfect regularity of function. The universe and every existence in the universe is characterized by harmony, order and perfect regularity.

What then is characterized by disharmony, disorder and imperfection, irregularity? Here 'Abdu'l-Bahá turns the argument back on its denier. For the source of disharmony, disorder, imper-

---

[130] Ibid.
[131] Ibid., 107
[132] SWAB 47

fection and irregularity is not the creation of God but the choice of man, not the universe but rather the denier himself. For human

> "capacity is of two kinds: innate and acquired. The innate capacity, which is the creation of God, is wholly and entirely good—in the innate nature there is no evil. The acquired capacity, however, can become the cause of evil."[133]

Through the acquired capacity, that is, education (environmental influence in all of its aspects and manifestations and instrumentalities),

> "two aspects: one divine and one satanic—that is, it is capable of both the greatest perfection and the greatest deficiency. Should it acquire virtues, it is the noblest of all things; and should it acquire vices, it becomes the most vile."[134] Because of the "satanic", the "world of man is sick."[135]

This sickness is not from God, it is from man. Evil is not from God, it is from man. Man's sickness, no matter how grave, is not hopeless, for God has provided a physician for man's ailment, a doctor who can prescribe the remedies for man's diseases.

> "Every divine Manifestation is the very life of the world, and the skilled physician of every ailing soul. The world of man is sick, and that competent Physician knoweth the cure, arising as He doth with teachings, counsels and admonishments that are the remedy for every pain, the healing balm to every wound."[136]

That one is a "madman" indeed who rejects the cure, the remedy from his Creator! Furthermore, there are consequences for

---

[133] SAQ IV:57.9
[134] SAQ III:36.5
[135] SWAB 59
[136] Ibid.

such a denial, such a rejection. While the denier may refuse to take responsibility for the consequences of his rebellion which is also a rejection of reality, of the divine order of things, inasmuch as *"the canopy of world order is upraised upon the two pillars of reward and punishment."*[137]

> "For rewards and punishments are said to be of two kinds—one being existential rewards and punishments and the other, ultimate rewards and punishments. Existential paradise and hell are to be found in all the worlds of God, whether in this world or in the heavenly realms of the spirit, and to gain these rewards is to attain life eternal."[138]

The denier, the rejectionist, the diseased one, the outlaw does not escape the consequences of his rebellion. Nor is he deprived of opportunities to be cured, healed, restored to harmony with the rest of the universe and with his Creator.

NINTH PROOF: SMALLEST CREATION PROVES EXISTENCE OF CREATOR

> "Likewise, throughout the world of existence the smallest created thing attests to the existence of a creator. For instance, this piece of bread attests that it has a maker."[139]

This argument we have already encountered in the course of studying the Eighth Proof, namely the assertion that "the part is an indication of the whole",[140] an example of inductive logic. The other connotations of this proof have been treated in the Second Proof.

---

[137] Baha'u'lláh. *Ishraqat*, in TB:126
[138] SAQ IV:60.2
[139] SAQ I:2.6
[140] SW XIV:4, 106; reprint in *Tablet to Dr. Forel*, p. 20

The original argument to be encountered here is that every created thing is a proof of the existence of God, and hence there are truly innumerable proofs, and the smallest created thing cannot be discounted. For every created thing reveals God and this is its real value. A piece of bread has a maker—s/he is called "baker". If "the part is the indication of the whole" then it follows that the universe has a maker—it is called "God". Also, a piece of bread has a maker, this is universally recognized. Who is that maker of the bread? The baker. The baker is the cook who mixed the ingredients and baked them in an oven. Who made the oven? Who made the ingredients? If we follow all of these leads to their sources, those sources will eventually converge upon one Source, one Maker of makers, and this we call God.

TENTH PROOF: LAWS OF NATURE ARE PROOFS OF THE EXISTENCE OF THE CREATOR

> "Hence it is clear that nature, in its very essence, is in the grasp of God's might, and that it is that Eternal and Almighty One Who subjects nature to ideal laws and organizing principles, and Who rules over it."[141]

The Tenth Proof can be inferred from this statement of 'Abdu'l-Bahá, and also from this passage from the Lawh-i-Hikmat of Bahá'u'lláh:

> "Say: Nature in its essence is the embodiment of My Name, the Maker, the Creator. Its manifestations are diversified by varying causes, and in this diversity there are signs for men of discernment. Nature is God's Will and is its expression in and through the contingent world. It is a dispensation of Providence ordained by the Ordainer, the All-Wise. Were anyone to affirm that it is the Will of God as manifested in the world of being, no

---

[141] SAQ I:1.7

one should question this assertion. It is endowed with a power whose reality men of learning fail to grasp. Indeed a man of insight can perceive naught therein save the effulgent splendour of Our Name, the Creator. Say: This is an existence which knoweth no decay, and Nature itself is lost in bewilderment before its revelations, its compelling evidences and its effulgent glory which have encompassed the universe."[142]

"There are two Books: one is the Book of creation and the other is the written Book. The written Book consisteth of the heavenly Books which are revealed to the Prophets of God...The Book of creation is the preserved Tablet and the outspread Roll of existence. The Book of Creation is in accord with the Written Book."[143]

Thomas Aquinas and Sir Isaac Newton were proponents of this proof, but 'Abdu'l-Bahá does not elaborate on it in any of his writings or talks currently available in English.

ELEVENTH PROOF: CHANGE IN CREATION PROVES EXISTENCE OF CREATOR

"Gracious God! The change in the outward form of the smallest thing proves the existence of a creator: Then how could this vast, boundless universe have created itself and come to exist solely through the mutual interaction of the elements? How patently false is such a notion!"[144] Again, as in the Ninth Proof, it is emphasized that quantity, volume, size does not determine

---

[142] Bahá'u'lláh. *Lawh-i-Hikmat*, in TB:141
[143] From a *Tablet of 'Abdu'l-Bahá*, in Bahiyyih Nakhjávání, *Response*. Oxford, George Ronald, 1981, p. 13 (Persian original in *Makátíb-i-'Abdu'l-Bahá*, 1:436–7); cited https://bahai-studies.ca/wp-content/uploads/2014/03/QuestionsandBahaiStudies.pdf
[144] SAQ I:2.7

fundamental principles. The purpose of divine philosophy is not to impress, to dazzle the reader, to seduce him by the voluptuousness or virility of proofs, nor to overwhelm him by the grandiosity or impenetrability of arguments. Rather the purpose of 'Abdu'l-Bahá is to unfold "the wisdom and knowledge of God, the effulgence of the Sun of Truth, the revelation of reality and divine philosophy."[145]

"The intellectual proofs of Divinity are based upon observation and evidence which constitute decisive argument, logically proving the reality of Divinity, the effulgence of mercy, the certainty of inspiration and immortality of the spirit."[146]

Even the least change in the smallest thing proves the existence of God. This is most logical, for after all, if every creation of God proves His existence then surely the smallest thing is as much of a proof as the largest. Furthermore, while many human beings are inclined to remember their Creator in times of great change, particularly when that change affects them personally and adversely, this argument points out that the most minor changes in the smallest of existences prove the point. How is it that change, any change at all proves the existence of God? Can anything change of itself, of its own will?

The least change is motivated by an agent of change, the least movement by a mover. In following the chain of movement and movers one must finally arrive at a prime changer or prime mover, for "to maintain that this process goes on indefinitely is manifestly absurd."[147] Also, inasmuch as every movement, every change in any existence implies the entire series of its antecedents, it also requires the existence of a prime mover, the source of change. Perhaps the first place that this argument was articulated

---

[145] PUP 326
[146] PUP 326
[147] SW XIV:4, 105; reprinted in *Tablet to Dr. Forel*, pp. 18–19

is in Aristotle's Metaphysics.[148] It is an alternative formulation of the "cosmological argument" which we encounter next.

TWELFTH PROOF: NECESSITY OF PRIMAL CAUSE

"Furthermore, although all created beings grow and develop, yet are they subjected to influences from without. For instance, the sun giveth heat, the rain nourisheth, the wind bringeth life, so that man can develop and grow. Thus it is clear that the human body is under influences from the outside, and that without those influences man could not grow. And likewise, those outside influences are subjected to other influences in their turn. For example, the growth and development of a human being is dependent upon the existence of water, and water is dependent upon the exsitence of rain, and rain is dependent upon the existence of clouds, and clouds are dependent upon the existence of the sun, which causeth land and sea to produce vapour, the condensation of vapour forming the clouds. Thus each one of these entities exerteth its influence and is likewise influenced in its turn. Inescapably then, the process leadeth to One Who influenceth all, and yet is influenced by none, thus severing the chain."[149]

"As we, however, reflect with broad minds upon this infinite universe, we observe that motion without a motive force, and an effect without a cause are both impossible; that every being hath come to exist under numerous influences and continually undergoeth reaction. These influences too are formed under the action of still other influences. For instance, plants grow and flourish through the outpourings of vernal showers, whilst the cloud itself

---

[148] Aristotle. *Metaphysics*. Beta, 4, 999b
[149] SWAB 49

is formed under various other agencies and these agencies in their turn are reacted upon by still other agencies. For example, plants and animals grow and develop under the influence of what the philosophers of our day designate as hydrogen and oxygen and are reacted upon by the effects of these two elements; and these in turn are formed under still other influences. The same can be said of other beings whether they affect other things or [are] affected. Such a process of causation goes on, and to maintain that this process goes on indefinitely is manifestly absurd. Thus such a chain of causation must of necessity lead eventually to Him who is the Ever-Living, the All-Powerful, who is Self-Dependent and the Ultimate Cause. This Universal Reality cannot be sensed, it cannot be seen. It must be so of necessity, for it is All-Embracing, not circumscribed, and such attributes qualify the effect and not the cause."[150]

The language of this Eleventh Proof as well as its reasoning is known to philosophy as the "cosmological argument", and as such its earliest recorded exponent seems to have been the Greek philosopher Plato, anticipated in Phaedrus[151] and developed in the Laws.[152] While this Eleventh Proof of divine philosophy is the only formal statement of this "cosmological argument", we have encountered other formulations thereof among the previously enumerated proofs. This is not an unusual or peculiar phenomena, inasmuch as Thomas Aquinas, the Catholic scholastic philosopher, in his Summa Theologia cites five proofs for the existence of God, the first three of which are varied formulations of the "cosmological argument". This is perhaps the most widely recognized of the proofs of Divinity, but it always bears re-statement. Just because something is not familiar does not mean that it is understood.

---

[150] SW XIV:4, 104–105; reprinted in *Tablet to Dr. Forel,* pp. 18–19
[151] Plato. *Phaedrus,* 245, C–E
[152] Plato. *Laws,* Book X.

'Abdu'l-Bahá does not merely make a formal statement or set forth a series of formal arguments. Rather are tangible examples referred to.

> "It is by the aid of such senses as those of sight, hearing, taste, smell and touch, that the mind comprehendeth, whereas, the soul is free from all agencies."[153]

'Abdu'l-Bahá describes the duality of knowledge in two contexts, illuminating in both cases:

> "Know that there are two kinds of knowledge: the knowledge of the essence of a thing and the knowledge of its attributes. The essence of each thing is known only through its attributes; otherwise, that essence is unknown and unfathomed. As our knowledge of things, even of created and limited ones, is of their attributes and not of their essence, how then can it be possible to understand in its essence the unbounded Reality of the Divinity? For the inner essence of a thing can never be known, only its attributes. For example, the inner reality of the sun is unknown, but it is understood through its attributes, which are heat and light. The inner essence of man is unknown and unfathomed, but it is known and characterized by its attributes. Thus everything is known by its attributes and not by its essence: Even though the human mind encompasses all things, and all outward things are in turn encompassed by it, yet the latter are unknown with regard to their essence and can only be known with regard to their attributes. How then can the ancient and everlasting Lord, Who is sanctified above all comprehension and imagining, be known in His Essence? That is, as created things can only be known through their attributes and not in their essence, the reality of the Divinity, too, must be un-

---

[153] SW XIV:4, 102; reprint in *Tablet to Dr. Forel*, p. 8

known with regard to its essence and known only with respect to its attributes."[154]

"There is a point that is pivotal to grasping the essence of the other questions that we have discussed or will be discussing, namely, that human knowledge is of two kinds. One is the knowledge acquired through the senses. That which the eye, the ear, or the senses of smell, taste, or touch can perceive is called "sensible". For example, the sun is sensible, as it can be seen. Likewise, sounds are sensible, as the ear can hear them; odours, as they can be inhaled and perceived by the sense of smell; foods, as the palate can perceive their sweetness, sourness, bitterness, or saltiness; heat and cold, as the sense of touch can perceive them. These are called sensible realities. The other kind of human knowledge is that of intelligible things; that is, it consists of intelligible realities which have no outward form or place and which are not sensible. For example, the power of the mind is not sensible, nor are any of the human attributes: These are intelligible realities. Love, likewise, is an intelligible and not a sensible reality. For the ear does not hear these realities, the eye does not see them, the smell does not sense them, the taste does not detect them, the touch does not perceive them. Even the ether, the forces of which are said in natural philosophy to be heat, light, electricity, and magnetism, is an intelligible and not a sensible reality. Likewise, nature itself is an intelligible and not a sensible reality; the human spirit is an intelligible and not a sensible reality."[155]

The examples, the "sensible realities" cited in the case of this Eleventh Proof are plant and animal existences and the human

---

[154] SAQ IV:59.3–3
[155] SAQ II:16, 1–3

body. These are the most immediate "sensible realities" that could be imagined, inasmuch as we experience most of life in our own bodies, and therefore are best acquainted with this example. As for plants and animals, we are surrounded by plants and animals and dependent upon both for our daily nourishment and most human beings spend a large portion of each day caring for plants and animals. In all three cases we know from personal experience that the plants will not grow without water, the water is not available without rain, the rain does not come unless there are clouds. We may not know from whence come the clouds or otherwise be able to follow this chain of causes any further than this, but we do know that each contingent reality is dependent upon others, that each is influenced by others, and that if there were no Cause of causes there would likewise be no effect of effects, and the plant, the animal and the body of man are the effects of many effects.

While this statement of the "cosmological argument" has been microcosmic and from the personal point of view of the average human being, another formulation is found in divine philosophy which is macrocosmic and from the overall perspective of the scientist:

> "For instance, we observe that the existence of beings is conditioned upon the coming together of various elements and their non-existence upon the decomposition of their constituent elements. For decomposition causes the dissociation of the various elements. Thus, as we observe [that] the coming together of elements giveth rise to the existence of beings, and knowing that beings are infinite, they being the effect, how can the Cause be finite?"[156]

The philosophers, other than Thomas Aquinas, who conceived of various formulations of the "cosmological argument"

---

[156] SW XIV:4, 105; reprinted in *Tablet to Dr. Forel*, p. 16

include Archbishop Anselm in his Monologion[157] and Rene Descartes in his Meditations[158] and his Principles of Philosophy.

THIRTEENTH PROOF: INFINITE UNIVERSE COULD NOT HAVE COME TO EXIST BY ITSELF

The divine philosopher asks "how could this vast, boundless universe have created itself and come to exist solely through the mutual interaction of the elements?"[159] The response to this question is the "teleological argument", also called the argument from design.

> "And as we reflect, we observe that man is like unto a tiny organism contained within a fruit; this fruit hath developed out of the blossom, the blossom hath grown out of the tree, the tree is sustained by the sap, and the sap formed out of earth and water. How then can this tiny organism comprehend the nature of the garden, conceive of the gardener and comprehend his being? This is manifestly impossible. Should that organism understand and reflect, it would observe that this garden, this tree, this blossom, this fruit would have in nowise have come to exist by themselves in such order and perfection. Similarly the wise and reflecting soul will know of a certainty that this infinite universe with all its grandeur and (perfect) order could not have come to exist by itself."[160]

Such an extraordinarily clear and concise and colorful "sensible figure" is this account that it immediately invites reaction and commentary. First of all, one is struck by the similarity of this formulation with the findings of ecological science, with the discovery that all organisms are inter-dependent, that they are irreplace-

---

[157] *Monologion*, Chapter 3

[158] *Meditations*, III.

[159] SAQ I:2.7

[160] SW XIV:4, 106; reprint in *Tablet to Dr. Forel*, p. 19

able parts of an ecosystem which operates in perfect harmony, balance and order. Secondly, this is an argument which appeals to aesthetics, to the admirer of beauty, and particularly to s/he who is attracted to the beauties of nature. The gardener can surely appreciate such a formulation, but the wilderness enthusiast as well. Thirdly, this argument strikes a chord with every person who has designed and built anything, for it will seem utterly absurd to any such person that a home, a bridge, a rock wall could have come into existence by itself. Indeed, every builder knows that what is left to itself will fall down and disintegrate. Fourthly, any person who has composed, cooked, weaved, knitted, potted, painted knows that the coming together of notes, of ingredients, of threads, of clay and water, of paints and canvass require an actor and that any beautiful creation requires that the actor have skill and intention.

> "Likewise every arrangement and formation that is not perfect in its order we designate as accidental, and that which is orderly, regular, perfect in its relations and every part of which is in its proper place and is the essential requisite of the other constituent parts, this we call a composition formed through will and knowledge."[161]

Again, in reference to the universe, to the macrocosm:

> "There is no doubt that these infinite beings and the association of these diverse elements arranged in countless forms must have proceeded from a Reality that could in no wise be bereft of will or understanding, and this infinite composition cast into infinite forms must have been caused by an all-embracing Wisdom."[162]

One might add that this "all-embracing Wisdom" must love His creation, to have created it in such order, regularity, perfection and beauty, and that He must particularly love His creation

---

[161] SW XIV:4, 107; reprint in *Tablet to Dr. Forel*, p. 23
[162] Ibid., pp. 23–24

of man inasmuch as in man He has created the capacity to appreciate the order, regularity, perfection and beauty of all of His creation. This design argument is considered so obvious in divine philosophy that the denier of this argument is dismissed in these unflattering terms:

> "This none can dispute save he that is obstinate and stubborn, and denieth the clear and unmistakable evidence, and becometh the object of the blessed Verse: 'deaf, dumb, blind and shall return no more.'"[163]

The first statement of the "teleological argument" may be found in Plato, and since him there have been many formulations of this proof.

The principle stumbling block for most students of this proof is over the problem of evil. The British philosopher John Stuart Mill in his Nature and Utility of Religion is not the first or the most recent of those who has denied the existence of God on the grounds of the defective, the imperfect nature of the universe, but his objections are cited inasmuch as they are forcefully and succinctly expressed:

> "For how stands the fact? That next to the greatness of these cosmic forces, the quality which most forcibly strikes everyone who does not avert his eyes from it is their perfect and absolute recklessness. They go straight to their end, without regarding what or whom they crush on the road."[164]

He cites hurricanes, crop failures, locust "plagues", shipwrecks, disease.

The response of 'Abdu'l-Bahá to this question of evil has already been touched on but will be cited in full:

> "Briefly, intelligible realities such as the praiseworthy attributes and perfections of man are purely good and

---

[163] Ibid.
[164] John Stuart Mill. *Nature and Utility of Religion.* 1874, p. 28

have a positive existence. Evil is simply their non-existence. So ignorance is the want of knowledge, error is the want of guidance, forgetfulness is the want of remembrance, foolishness is the want of understanding: All these are nothing in themselves and have no positive existence."[165]

In divine philosophy, there is in reality no evil, no ignorance, no error, no forgetfulness, no stupidity—these things do not have real existence, they represent merely the absence, the lack of positive qualities. But does the suffering that is caused by these non-realities, by evil, ignorance, error, forgetfulness and stupidity, that is, by the absence of good, knowledge, guidance, memory and good sense, is that suffering also unreal? Is suffering the lack of joy, the absence of happiness? Let us continue:

"As for sensible realities, these are also purely good, and evil is merely their non-existence; that is, blindness is the want of sight, deafness is the want of hearing, poverty is the want of wealth, illness is the want of health, death is the want of life, and weakness is the want of strength."[166]

Likewise, it may be asked, is the suffering caused by the want of sight, of hearing, of wealth, of health, of life, of strength real or unreal? But still to continue:

"Now, a doubt comes to mind: Scorpions and snakes are poisonous—is this good or evil, for they have a positive existence? Yes, it is true that scorpions and snakes are evil, but only in relation to us and not to themselves, for their venom is their weapon and their sting their means of defense. But as the constituent elements of their venom are incompatible with those of our bodies—that is, as these constituent elements are mutually

---

[165] SAQ V:74.3
[166] SAQ V:74.4

opposed—the venom is evil, or rather, those elements are evil in relation to each other, while in their own reality they are both good."[167]

There is only evil in the relations between existences then? Evil of one thing in relation to another? But then is there not evil in the relation between human beings and the non-existence of such intellectual realities as good, knowledge, guidance, memory and stupidity; and such sensible realities as sight, hearing, wealth, health, life and strength?

"To summarize, one thing may be evil in relation to another but not evil within the limits of its own being. It follows therefore that there is no evil in existence: Whatsoever God has created, He has created good. Evil consists merely in non-existence. For example, death is the absence of life: When man is no longer sustained by the power of life, he dies. Darkness is the absence of light: When light is no more, darkness reigns. Light is a positively existing thing, but darkness has no positive existence; it is merely its absence. Likewise, wealth is a positively existing thing but poverty is merely its absence."[168]

The evil of one thing in relation to another is not absolute, that is, in and of itself and hence it is unreal. Perhaps in other words, a man may experience another reality in relationship to himself as evil, but this does not make that reality evil. That other reality is good, even as that man is good. How can it be that he experiences another reality (or even his own reality) as evil when in and of itself it is good? It is that man's perception which perceives evil where there is good, which mistakes evil for good. We have already briefly encountered this argument regarding perception, but it will be cited in more detail to explain this question of evil so that it will not remain a stumbling block for recognition of the proofs of Divinity.

---

[167] SAQ V:74.5
[168] SAQ V:74.6

Divine philosophy reveals that

> "capacity is of two kinds: innate and acquired. The innate capacity, which is the creation of God, is wholly and entirely good—in the innate nature there is no evil. The acquired capacity, however, can become the cause of evil."[169]

Furthermore,

> "But this human spirit has two aspects: one divine and one satanic—that is, it is capable of both the greatest perfection and the greatest deficiency. Should it acquire virtues, it is the noblest of all things; and should it acquire vices, it becomes the most vile."[170]

Even as the innate nature of man is good, therefore if he develops that innate nature he will perceive good in himself and in all of creation, and he will do so not by remaining without education and influence and training—for this is impossible inasmuch as everything in his environment will inevitably have an influence upon him—but rather by acquiring virtues and becoming "the noblest of all beings". The closer he comes to perceiving the good in all things, the closer he comes to manifesting the divine nature with which God has endowed him.

Attainment to this knowledge is described by Bahá'u'lláh as follows:

> "Gazing with the eye of absolute insight, the wayfarer in this valley seeth in God's creation neither contradiction nor incongruity, and at every moment exclaimeth, "No defect canst thou see in the creation of the God of mercy. Repeat the gaze: Seest thou a single flaw?" [Qur'án 67:3] He beholdeth justice in injustice, and in justice, grace. In ignorance he findeth many a knowledge hidden, and in knowledge a myriad wisdoms mani-

---

[169] SAQ IV:57.9
[170] SAQ III:36.5

95

> fest…Yet those who journey in the garden land of true
> knowledge, since they see the end in the beginning, be-
> hold peace in war and conciliation in enmity."[171]

What is suffering? Suffering consists in attachment to and love of what has changed and the wish that change had not occurred. For there is no suffering for one who accepts his life with radiant acquiescence. It is not what has happened to one, the influences from outside that determine whether or not one has lived well, whether or not one has chosen the satanic or the angelic path; it is one's response to those influences. A hurricane, earthquake, shipwreck, all of these acts of nature are good in themselves, and if they cause deaths, those deaths are merely the cessation of lives. There is nothing evil in the cessation of life if it comes through an act of nature. God gives life and God takes it away—this is for Him to do. "He doeth whatsoever He willeth." What sort of life did those live who died as a result of acts of nature? That is the important question, for them. What sort of lives do we live, each one of us, in response to our individual circumstances? That is the important question, for us.

> "For example, God has created all men in such a fashion,
> and has given them such a capacity and disposition, that
> they are benefited by sugar and honey and are harmed
> or killed by poison. This is an innate capacity and dispo-
> sition that God has bestowed equally upon all men. But
> man may begin little by little to take poison by ingest-
> ing a small quantity every day and gradually increasing
> it until he reaches the point where he would perish if
> he were not to consume several grams of opium every
> day, and where his innate capacities are completely sub-
> verted. Consider how the innate capacity and disposi-
> tion can be so completely changed, through variation

---

[171] Baha'u'lláh, *Seven Valleys* [SV], 1856, new translation online at: https://www.bahai.org/library/authorita-tive-texts/bahaullah/call-divine-beloved/4#639859466

of habit and training, as to be entirely perverted. It is not on account of their innate capacity and disposition that one reproaches the wicked, but rather on account of that which they themselves have acquired.

"In the innate nature of things there is no evil—all is good. This applies even to certain apparently blameworthy attributes and dispositions which seem inherent in some people, but which are not in reality reprehensible. For example, you can see in a nursing child, from the beginning of its life, the signs of greed, of anger, and of ill temper; and so it might be argued that good and evil are innate in the reality of man, and that this is contrary to the pure goodness of the innate nature and of creation. The answer is that greed, which is to demand ever more, is a praiseworthy quality provided that it is displayed under the right circumstances. Thus, should a person show greed in acquiring science and knowledge, or in the exercise of compassion, high-mindedness, and justice, this would be most praiseworthy. And should he direct his anger and wrath against the bloodthirsty tyrants who are like ferocious beasts, this too would be most praiseworthy. But should he display these qualities under other conditions, this would be deserving of blame.

"It follows therefore that in existence and creation there is no evil at all, but that when man's innate qualities are used in an unlawful way, they become blameworthy. Thus if a wealthy and generous person gives alms to a poor man to spend on his necessities, and if the latter spends that sum in an improper way, that is blameworthy. The same holds true of all the innate qualities of man which constitute the capital of human life: If they are displayed and employed in an improper way, they become blameworthy. It is clear then that the innate nature is purely good.

"Consider that the worst of all qualities and the most odious of all attributes, and the very foundation of all evil, is lying, and that no more evil or reprehensible quality can be imagined in all existence. It brings all human perfections to naught and gives rise to countless vices. There is no worse attribute than this, and it is the foundation of all wickedness. Now, all this notwithstanding, should a physician console a patient and say, "Thank God, you are doing better and there is hope for your recovery", although these words may be contrary to the truth, yet sometimes they will ease the patient's mind and become the means of curing the illness. And this is not blameworthy."[172]

It may be asserted that evil is a proof of the existence of God. For inasmuch as evil is actually the absence of good, and inasmuch as all existences are objectively good, the source of all that good must be superlatively good. However, we are warned by 'Abdu'l-Bahá not to indulge in vain imaginings:

"As to the attributes and perfections such as will, knowledge, power and other ancient attributes that we ascribe to that Divine Reality, these are the signs that reflect the existence of beings in the visible plane and not the absolute perfections of the Divine Essence that cannot be comprehended."[173]

---

[172] SAQ IV: 57.9–12
[173] SW XIV:4, 104; reprint as *Tablet to Dr. Forel*, p. 17

FOURTEENTH PROOF: THE UNIVERSE HAS A PURPOSE AND HENCE A CREATOR

"All divine philosophers and men of wisdom and under-standing, when observing these endless beings, have considered that in this great and infinite universe all things end in the mineral kingdom, that the outcome of the mineral kingdom is the vegetable kingdom, the out-come of the vegetable kingdom is the animal kingdom and the outcome of the animal kingdom the world of man. The consummation of this limitless universe with all its grandeur and glory hath been man himself, who in this world of being toileth and suffereth for a time, with diverse ills and pains, and ultimately disintegrates, leaving no trace and no fruit after him. Were it so, there is no doubt that this infinite universe with all its per-fections has ended in sham and delusion with no result, no fruit, no permanence and no effect. It would be ut-terly without meaning. They (the philosophers) were thus convinced that such is not the case, that this Great Workshop with all its power, its bewildering magnifi-cence and endless perfections, cannot eventually come to naught. That still another life should exist is thus certain, and, just as the vegetable kingdom is unaware of the world of man, so we, too, know not of the Great Life hereafter that followeth the life of man here below. Our non-comprehension of that life, however, is no proof of its non-existence. The mineral world, for instance, is utterly unaware of the world of man and cannot com-prehend it, but the ignorance of a thing is no proof of its non-existence. Numerous and conclusive proofs exist that go to show that this infinite world cannot end with this human life."[174]

---

[174] SW XIV:4, 104; reprint in *Tablet to Dr. Forel*, pp. 13–14

While this passage at first reading may not seem to reveal a proof for the existence of God, study yielded more than could have been anticipated. First of all, we are already familiar with the argument:

> "consider machinery and workshops and the interaction existing among the various component parts and sections, and how connected they are one with the other. All these relations and interactions, however, are connected with a central power which is their motive force, their pivot and their source."[175]

The Great Workshop of the universe is linked to the Twelfth Proof another proof for the existence of God. Secondly, we find in two formulations the statement that the ignorance or non-comprehension of a thing is no proof of its non-existence. This is a particularly significant maxim, appealing quite universally to philosophers and scientists alike. Can the opposite be affirmed with the same degree of appeal to the rational mind, that the knowledge and comprehension of a thing is no proof of its existence? Yes, it can, for there is much knowledge and much comprehension that is false and fictitious rather than grounded in reality. Both of these assertions point to proofs of Divinity—the first to the consideration of proofs for the existence of God, for why otherwise would we bother to investigate a phenomenon which we agree we cannot experience directly; the second to the careful study of each argument in support of the existence of such a phenomenon, inasmuch as we do not want to be duped, to be misled into acceptance of an untruth. Thirdly this passage clearly formulates a proof for the existence of the Great Life hereafter; it also implies a proof for the existence of God—one based upon meaning. Without an afterlife there is no meaning for the terrestrial life of man. Without a Creator there is no meaning for the existence of the universe. Why would man exist with meaning, why would the universe exist with meaning if it were not willed into exis-

---

[175] SW XIV:4, 107; reprint in *Tablet to Dr. Forel*, p. 23

tence by a Creator, and not just any creator, but the superlative of superlatives?

> "For instance, as we consider created things we observe infinite perfections, and the created things being in the utmost regularity and perfection we infer that the Ancient Power on whom dependeth the existence of these beings, cannot be ignorant; thus we say He is All-Knowing. It is certain that it is not impotent, it must be All-Powerful; it is not poor, it must be All-Possessing; it is not non-existent, it must be Ever-Living."[176]

This is a variation of the "teleological argument" but with a new feature—for the universe does not only require a Creator because of its design, its order, its beauty, but it also requires a Creator because it has meaning, it has purpose. Meaning requires intention, not only intention revealed in the universe itself but intention revealed for the universe. The meaning of the mineral is not just to be a mineral but to become the vegetable; likewise the vegetable's meaning is fulfilled in the animal; and the animal's meaning is revealed in man. What is man's meaning? His meaning is to know and love God, to recognize and serve his Creator. This is stated in so many different contexts and phrases that it does not require citation. Man would thus be without meaning if he could not know and love his Creator, and if his Creator did not exist he would thus be without meaning.

FIFTEENTH PROOF: BOUNTIES OF GOD PROVE HIS EXISTENCE

> "But the question may be asked, 'How shall we know God?' We know Him by His attributes. We know Him by His signs. We know Him by His names. We know not what the reality of the sun is. But we know the sun by the ray,

---

[176] SW XIV:4, 105; reprinted in *Tablet to Dr. Forel*, p. 17

> by the heat, by its efficacy, by its penetration. By the bounty and effulgence of the sun we recognize the sun, but as to what constitutes the reality of the solar energy, that is unknowable to us. But the attributes characterizing the sun are knowable. If we wish to come in touch with the reality of divinity, we do so by recognizing its phenomena, its attributes and traces which are widespread in the universe. All things in the world of phenomena are expressive of that one reality. Its lights are shining, its heat is manifest, its power is expressive and its education or training resplendent everywhere. What proof could there be greater than that of its functioning, or its attributes which are manifest?...Hence we can observe the traces and attributes of God which are resplendent in all phenomena and shining as the sun at midday, and know surely that these emanate from an infinite source."[177]

This may be called the Sun Proof inasmuch as it uses the symbol, the image of the sun to demonstrate the ways in which God is known. We do not know the sun—it is millions of miles away from us; if we got much closer to it we would be incinerated; its intensity and power in themselves prevent us from approaching. At the same time, we know a great deal about the sun from its influence, its attributes, its signs, its "names". It influences all organic creation through its light, its heat, its gravitational force. Without the sun there would be no organic life as we know it. Without the sun we would not exist. Yet we only know the sun by its effects. This image, this symbol is found in widely diverse sources, as Apollo in Greek myth, Indra in Vedantic myth, Ra and briefly Aton in Egyptian myth, the pillar of fire and the burning bush in the Torah, emblem of the Shah of Iran, and cited in the holy scriptures of Zoroastrianism, Judaism and Hinduism in its manifestations as the supernal inner light. Many schools of mys-

---

[177] PUP 422, 423

ticism likewise have recourse to this living symbol to indicate the inaccessible reaches of Reality, and its rays as the spiritual super-structure of all existences. The traces, effects, influences, attributes and signs of God are as ubiquitous in the universe as are the light and heat and gravitational force of the sun. This is an affirmation which will require further study and examples will have to be identified in all ranks of creation to demonstrate the truth of this proof to the skeptic.

We are familiar however with the notion of knowing something only by its effects.

"For instance, the nature of ether is unknown, but that it existeth is certain by the effects it produceth, heat, light and electricity being the waves thereof. And as we consider the outpourings of Divine Grace we are assured of the existence of God."[178]

"Similarly in the world of being there exist forces unseen by the eye such as the force of ether previously mentioned, that cannot be sensed, that cannot be seen. However from the effects it produceth, that is from its waves and vibrations, light, heat, electricity appear and are made evident.

"In like manner is the power of growth, of feeling, of understanding, of thought, of memory, of imagination and of discernment; all these inner faculties are unseen of the eye and cannot be sensed, yet all are evident by the effects they produce."[179]

"It is the mind that is the all-unifying agency that so uniteth all the component parts one with the other...

---

[178] SW XIV:4, 105; reprint in *Tablet to Dr. Forel*, p. 16. The existence of ether was still widely regarded as supported by science at the time of the writing of this Tablet, and it was cited as an example of something believed to exist which is nevertheless not directly perceived, but rather inferred from "the effects it produceth".

[179] SW XIV:4, 106; reprinted in *Tablet to Dr. Forel*, pp. 19–20

and though that all-unifying agency in the temple of man be not sensed or seen and the reality thereof be unknown, yet by its effects it manifesteth itself with the greatest power."[180]

"Sensible realities are those which are perceived by the five outer senses: So, for example, those outward things which the eye sees are called sensible. Intelligible realities are those which have no outward existence but are perceived by the mind. For example, the mind itself is an intelligible reality and has no outward existence. Likewise, all human virtues and attributes have an intelligible rather than a sensible existence; that is, they are realities that are perceived by the mind and not by the senses."[181]

This is not for a moment to suggest that the human mind can understand the reality of every insensible thing, or that everything that is not sensible is intellectual.

"Man discerns only manifestations, or attributes, of objects, while the identity, or reality, of them remains hidden. For example, we call this object a flower. What do we understand by this name and title? We understand that the qualities appertaining to this organism are perceptible to us, but the intrinsic elemental reality, or identity, of it remains unknown. Its external appearance and manifest attributes are knowable; but the inner being, the underlying reality or intrinsic identity, is still beyond the ken and perception of our human powers. Inasmuch as the realities of material phenomena are impenetrable and unknowable and are only apprehended through their properties or qualities, how much more this is true concerning the reality of

---

[180] SW XIV:4, 106–107; reprinted in *Tablet to Dr. Forel*, p. 21
[181] SAQ V:74.2

Divinity, that holy essential reality which transcends the plane and grasp of mind and man? That which comes within human grasp is finite, and in relation to it we are infinite because we can grasp it. Assuredly, the finite is lesser than the infinite; the infinite is ever greater. If the reality of Divinity could be contained within the grasp of human mind, it would after all be possessed of an intellectual existence only—a mere intellectual concept without extraneous existence, an image or likeness which had come within the comprehension of finite intellect. The mind of man would be transcendental thereto. How could it be possible that an image which has only intellectual existence is the reality of Divinity, which is infinite? Therefore, the reality of Divinity in its identity is beyond the range of human intellection because the human mind, the human intellect, the human thought are limited, whereas the reality of Divinity is unlimited. How can the limited grasp the unlimited and transcend it? Impossible. The unlimited always comprehends the limited. The limited can never comprehend, surround nor take in the limited. Therefore, every concept of Divinity which has come within the intellection of a human being is finite, or limited, and is a pure product of imagination, whereas the reality of Divinity is holy and sacred above and beyond all such concepts."[182]

There are at least three important points to be studied here: First of all, that man is incapable of recognizing the existence of God through knowledge of the reality of Divinity; Secondly, that man is also incapable of conceiving of God, for God is not an intellectual reality, God transcends man and in order to intellectually conceive of God man would have to transcend God; Third, that all that is left for man is to recognize the existence of God

---

[182] PUP 421–422

through understanding His attributes as they are revealed in His creation.

Having come to a conclusion in this, the Mother Proof for the existence of God, divine philosophy proceeds to rank the emanations from God in the order of their manifestation of the names and attributes of God. Although all emanations from God reveal these names and attributes of God, they do not reveal them equally. At the lowest rank is the mineral, then the vegetable, then the animal, and the highest rank of the contingent world is the rank of man. Man is at the highest rank of materiality and the lowest rank of spirituality.

> "However, those who have thoroughly investigated the questions of divinity know of a certainty that the material worlds terminate at the end of the arc of descent; that the station of man lies at the end of the arc of descent and the beginning of the arc of ascent, which is opposite the Supreme Centre; and that from the beginning to the end of the arc of ascent the degrees of progress are of a spiritual nature. The arc of descent is called that of "bringing forth" and the arc of ascent that of "creating anew". The arc of descent ends in material realities and the arc of ascent in spiritual realities."[183]

SIXTEENTH PROOF: GRADATION IN ALL THINGS PROVES EXISTENCE OF GOD

This proof is regarded by some philosophers to be prefigured in Plato's conception of eternal forms, what might in contemporary parlance be designated as archetypes, and may be found in differing formulations, in Anselm's Monologion,[184] and in Thomas Aquinas, Summa Theologica.[185] 'Abdu'l-Bahá also affirms that all

---

[183] SAQ V:81.9
[184] *Anselm's Monologion,* chapter 4
[185] *Summa Theologica,* Third Article: the fourth way

things are designed and organized according to rank, and that this leads inexorably to One which is of the very highest rank, the greatest in truth, the greatest in being. He wrote:

> "...all existent beings are in their very nature created in ranks or degrees, for capacities are various..."[186] and "The preservation of different ranks or degrees is necessary."[187]

We have earlier seen the argument that things are proved by their opposites, but this is a new variation, which states that there is a ladder of existences, Jacob's ladder as it were, from the lowest to the most high, from the base to the sublime.

SEVENTEENTH PROOF: MORALITY REQUIRES THE EXISTENCE OF GOD

Again here is an argument which may first have been articulated by Plato, then repeated and amplified by Anselm in Monologion,[188] and then re-introduced by Immanuel Kant and much developed since then as the "moral argument". Essentially, if good exists there must be a highest good, and a source of all good, and this is God. From another perspective, if there is no God then there is no justification for morality; historically we know that without morality there is no beauty, no harmony, no coordination, no governance, and without these and other principles of civilization which are brought into being through the operation of morality there can be no personal or social integration; consequently, for the good of both the individual and the social man there must be morality, and if there is morality then there must be God.

'Abdu'l-Bahá calls upon each human being, who in being human is created a seeker of truth:

---

[186] SWAB 159:190
[187] SW XIX:11, February 1929, p. 347, *'Abdu'l-Bahá in America*, Chapter IX, by Dr. Díyá Baghdádí
[188] *Monologion,* chapters 1 and 2

> "apply thyself to rational and authoritative arguments.
> For arguments are a guide to the path and by this the
> heart is turned unto the Sun of Truth. And when the
> heart is turned unto the Sun, then the eye will be
> opened and will recognize the Sun through the Sun it-
> self."[189]

We have already considered some of the rational arguments in
favour of the existence of God.

EIGHTEENTH PROOF: ONTOLOGICAL PROOF

The "**ontological proof**" indicates that there must be a
Being greater than which no being can be imagined. St. Anselm,
Archbishop of Canterbury, 1033–1109 A.D. is credited with the
first articulation of this proof. It was reiterated by Descartes;
Spinoza and Leibniz.

> "This argument undertakes to deduce the existence of
> God from the idea of Him as the Infinite which is pres-
> ent to the human mind; but as already stated, theistic
> philosophers are not agreed as to the logical validity of
> this deduction."[190]

This is an understatement of the opposition to this proof.
Elsewhere the author of this article, which is representative of a
traditional Roman Catholic theological perspective, writes:

> "Hence the great majority of scholastic philosophers
> have rejected the ontological argument as propound-
> ed by St. Anselm and Descartes nor as put forward by
> Leibniz does it escape the difficulty that has been
> stated."[191]

---

[189] TAB I:168
[190] http://www.newadvent.org/cathen/06608b.htm#IBf
[191] Ibid.

The argument is circular in its reasoning, and it presumes that the human mind is capable of understanding the nature of God, a presumption that will be addressed shortly.

> "As stated by St. Anselm, the argument runs thus: The idea of God as the Infinite means the greatest Being that can be thought of, but unless actual existence outside the mind is included in this idea, God would not be the greatest conceivable Being since a Being that exists both in the mind as an object of thought, and outside the mind or objectively, would be greater than a Being that exists in the mind only; therefore God exists not only in the mind but outside of it. Descartes states the argument in a slightly different way as follows: Whatever is contained in a clear and distinct idea of a thing must be predicated of that thing; but a clear and distinct idea of an absolutely perfect Being contains the notion of actual existence; therefore since we have the idea of an absolutely perfect Being such a Being must really exist. To mention a third form of statement, Leibniz would put the argument thus: God is at least possible since the concept of Him as the Infinite implies no contradiction; but if He is possible He must exist because the concept of Him involves existence."[192]

'Abdu'l-Bahá did not think much of arguments that derive from theoretical conceptions of God. He wrote, for example, "This people, all of them, have pictured a god in the realm of the mind, and worship that image which they have made for themselves. And yet that image is comprehended, the human mind being the comprehender thereof, and certainly the comprehender is greater than that which lieth within its grasp; for imagination is but the branch, while mind is the root; and certainly the root is greater than the branch. Consider then, how all the peoples of the world are bowing the knee to a fancy of their own contriving,

---

[192] Ibid.

how they have created a creator within their own minds, and they call it the Fashioner of all that is—whereas in truth it is but an illusion. Thus are the people worshipping only an error of perception.

"But that Essence of Essences, that Invisible of Invisibles, is sanctified above all human speculation, and never to be overtaken by the mind of man. Never shall that immemorial Reality lodge within the compass of a contingent being. His is another realm, and of that realm no understanding can be won. No access can be gained thereto; all entry is forbidden there. The utmost one can say is that Its existence can be proved, but the conditions of Its existence are unknown.

> "That such an Essence doth exist, the philosophers and learned doctors one and all have understood; but whenever they tried to learn something of Its being, they were left bewildered and dismayed, and at the end, despairing, their hopes in ruins, they went their way, out of this life. For to comprehend the state and the inner mystery of that Essence of Essences, that Most Secret of Secrets, one needs must have another power and other faculties; and such a power, such faculties would be more than humankind can bear, wherefore no word of Him can come to them."[193]

NINETEENTH PROOF: COMMON CONSENT

There is a proof called the argument from common consent, known in Latin as consensus gentium. This argument would seek to prove the existence of God from the fact that belief in that existence is widespread, and that it spans vastly different and unconnected cultures at various levels of development. Some would argue, as a corollary of this proof, that in human nature there is an inherent tendency to attest to the existence

---

[193] SWAB 53–54

of God. Related to this argument is the proof from direct experience and the proof from miracles. Inasmuch as both of these proofs are spiritual rather than rational, they are discussed in the section devoted to spiritual proofs. They are also Scriptural, inasmuch as there are numerous references to direct experience and miracles in the Scriptures, and these will be duly noted as well.

When we consider that the argument from common consent depends upon complete confidence upon the validity of theological positions arrived at by consensus, this foray of the democratic principle into the realm of spiritual truth-seeking may be weighed in the scales of justice. It is facile of demonstration that often common consent has resulted in the most grave distortions of judgment and perception, as, for example, the embrace of an un-reasoning zenophobia, racialism and communism by millions of Chinese, Germans, Italians, Japanese, Russians and Turks during the 20th century, the catastrophic results of which are known to all of my readers. Common consent rests upon the psychological habit of imitation, which is not regarded as the appropriate foundation for either individual or collective decision-making by 'Abdu'l-Bahá. He wrote and spoke about the dangers and deleterious effects of "blind imitation" in instances too numerous to cite, a few of which are quoted here:

> "Release yourselves from this blind following of the bigots, this senseless imitation which is the principal reason why men fall away into paths of ignorance and degradation."[194]

> "Among these teachings was the independent investigation of reality so that the world of humanity may be saved from the darkness of imitation and attain to the truth; may tear off and cast away this ragged and outgrown garment of 1,000 years ago and may put on

---

[194] SDC 104

the robe woven in the utmost purity and holiness in the loom of reality."[195]

"And the breeding-ground of all these tragedies is prejudice: prejudice of race and nation, of religion, of political opinion; and the root cause of prejudice is blind imitation of the past—imitation in religion, in racial attitudes, in national bias, in politics. So long as this aping of the past persisteth, just so long will the foundations of the social order be blown to the four winds, just so long will humanity be continually exposed to direst peril."[196]

"From the continual imitation of ancient and worn-out ways, the world had grown dark as darksome night."[197]

TWENTIETH PROOF: UNIVERSAL ENACTMENT

'Abdu'l-Bahá has formulated a proof that resembles the argument from common consent, but which draws the circle of participation even wider than that argument, making it on universal enactment rather than common consent. Furthermore, it does not entrust the consent to the fickle human will, but instead depicts it as integral to human life, inescapable and inherent in our very existence. In one of his Tablets he writes:

"Thou hast written of a verse in the Gospels, asking if at the time of Christ all souls did hear His call. Know that faith is of two kinds. The first is objective faith that is expressed by the outer man, obedience of the limbs and senses. The other faith is subjective, and unconscious obedience to the will of God. There is no doubt that, in the day of a Manifestation such as Christ, all contingent

[195] 'Abdu'l-Bahá. *Tablet to the Hague*, p. 4
[196] SWAB 247
[197] SWAB 252

beings possessed subjective faith and had unconscious obedience to His Holiness Christ.

"For all parts of the creational world are of one whole. Christ the Manifestor reflecting the divine Sun represented the whole. All the parts are subordinate and obedient to the whole. The contingent beings are the branches of the tree of life while the Messenger of God is the root of that tree. The branches, leaves and fruit are dependent for their existence upon the root of the tree of life. This condition of unconscious obedience constitutes subjective faith. But the discerning faith that consists of true knowledge of God and the comprehension of divine words, of such faith there is very little in any age. That is why His Holiness Christ said to His followers, 'Many are called but few are chosen.'"[198]

Extrapolating from this statement, "subjective faith" which consists of "unconscious obedience" to the Manifestation of God in His Day, and hence "unconscious obedience to the Will of God" is a proof of the existence of God for all human beings. Hence, in discovering and adhering to proofs of the Divine we are becoming conscious of what was always there. Whereas we were blind, now we see. Whereas we were deaf, now we hear. Whereas we were heedless, we become aware. This theme of "awakening" from a sleeping or intoxicated or otherwise compromised capacity of perception is found in the writings and talks of 'Abdu'l-Bahá, including these two passages:

"Consequently, when thou traversest the regions of the world, thou shalt conclude that all progress is the result of association and co-operation, while ruin is the outcome of animosity and hatred. Notwithstanding this,

---

[198] 'Abdu'l-Bahá, in *Bahá'í World Faith* [BWF], p. 364. The source of this passage, cited by Horace Holley, the compiler of this collection of Bahá'í texts, has not been located. Hence the authenticity of this text is in doubt.

the world of humanity doth not take warning, nor doth it awake from the slumber of heedlessness. Man is still causing differences, quarrels and strife in order to marshal the cohorts of war and, with his legions, rush into the field of bloodshed and slaughter."[199]

"Their divines, having concluded that all those essential qualifications of humankind set forth in the Holy Book were by then a dead letter, began to think only of furthering their own selfish interests, and afflicted the people by allowing them to sink into the lowest depths of heedlessness and ignorance."[200]

TWENTY-FIRST PROOF: GRANDEUR OF THE UNIVERSE PROOVES EXISTENCE OF CREATOR

It is not just the creation that proves the existence of a Creator... but the grandeur, the magnificence of the creation is sufficient proof of His existence. This proof is also implied in another statement of 'Abdu'l-Bahá:

"All these majestic scenes of nature, in reality, prove the greatness of the Creator and the antiquity of the world. This globe is indeed millions of years old, and its Creator has had no beginning and will have no ending. He has been, is and will be the Alpha and Omega. A creator presupposes creatures, just as light presupposes the existence of the sun."[201]

The great Jewish philosopher Abraham Heschel cited this as the first proof of God in an article by George F. Thomas[202]:

[199] SWAB 289

[200] 'Abdu'l-Bahá. *The Secret of Divine Civilization* [SDC], p. 77

[201] SW X:10, 203 (8 September 1919)

[202] George F. Thomas. "Philosophy and theology," *Theology Today, 30* (3), 1973, pp. 273–274. Retrieved October 2004, from http://theologytoday.ptsem.edu/oct1973/v30-3-article8.htm.

"The first way, personal insight, is awareness here and now of the grandeur of the world around us which points beyond itself to God. We sense grandeur or sublimity in natural beauty and acts of goodness, and through them we are aware of a meaning that is greater than themselves. The spontaneous response to them is wonder, "perpetual surprise," unless we have become indifferent to their grandeur by taking them for granted. Both the common things of nature and man's own being which is "fearfully and marvelously made"[203] evoke wonder. As Kant said, the mind is filled with "admiration and awe" at "the starry heavens above and the moral law within." Moreover, as we stand before the mystery of the universe, awe is awakened in us.[204] However well we may think we know things as they appear to our senses, they remain unknown to us in their essence. Although God is not the mystery but the meaning beyond the mystery, awe before it is an awareness of something transcendent to the world and yet present in it. Awe and reverence, therefore, are "the root of faith".[205] The whole earth is full of God's glory, which is his presence, but we are blind to it because our lives are dominated by routine and our hearts have become callous.[206] Hence, a recovery of awe and reverence is a necessary condition of the renewal of faith.

"But this is only the beginning. For religion is not wonder at the grandeur and awe before the mystery of the world, it is "the result of what man does" with his wonder and awe. We have the awareness that a question is addressed to us from our experience: "What is the

---

[203] Psalm 139:14
[204] Abraham Joshua Heschel. *God in Search of Man*. New York: Jewish Publication Society, 1955, p. 55
[205] Ibid., p. 77
[206] Ibid., p. 85

meaning of the mystery of the world?".[207] Faith arises as a response to this question. It is "an act of freedom" which goes beyond our limited faculties of reason and perception and does not depend upon speculation and proof. It is an answer to the question addressed to us by the grandeur and mystery of the universe and arises in "moments of insight." However, these moments are "rare events" in our experience and the immediate certainty we attain from them "does not retain its intensity" after they are gone.[208] It is remembrance of these moments of insight and loyalty to our response in them that sustains our faith. "In this sense, faith is faithfulness."[209]

"In following this way to God through personal insight and faith man must take the initiative but God's aid is necessary. "Without God's aid," says Heschel, "man cannot find him. Without man's seeking, his aid is not granted".[210]

"God concludes but we must commence".[211]

Similarly, while we have the ability to obey God's commandments, we can count on God's help and his compassion for our moral failures. This is Heschel's answer to the problem of human freedom and divine grace. "God is not indifferent to man's quest for him," so man's search for God is met by God's search for man."

Bahá'u'lláh attests to God reaching out to man, writing:

"For whereas in days past every lover besought and searched after his Beloved, it is the Beloved Himself

---

[207] Ibid., p. 110
[208] Ibid., p. 132
[209] Ibid.
[210] Ibid., p. 146
[211] Ibid., p. 147

Who now is calling His lovers and is inviting them to attain His presence."[212]

The reciprocity of the relationship between God and man is furthermore espoused in some of the Hidden Words:

"3. O SON OF MAN!
Veiled in My immemorial being and in the ancient eternity of My essence, I knew My love for thee; therefore I created thee, have engraved on thee Mine image and revealed to thee My beauty.

"4. O SON OF MAN!
I loved thy creation, hence I created thee. Wherefore, do thou love Me, that I may name thy name and fill thy soul with the spirit of life.

"5. O SON OF BEING!
Love Me, that I may love thee. If thou lovest Me not, My love can in no wise reach thee. Know this, O servant."[213]

TWENTY-SECOND PROOF:
PROBABLE AND PRAGMATIC

We may infer from this passage from one of the Tablets of Bahá'u'lláh, that belief in God (and explicitly belief in the afterlife) is beneficial to human existence[214]:

"The majority of the truly wise and learned have, throughout the ages, as it hath been recorded by the Pen of Glory in the Tablet of Wisdom, borne witness to the truth of that which the holy Writ of God hath revealed. Even the materialists have testified in their writings to the wisdom of these divinely-appointed

---

[212] Bahá'u'lláh. *Gleanings*, CLI, p. 320
[213] Baha'u'lláh. *Arabic Hidden Words*
[214] GL LXXXI:158

Messengers, and have regarded the references made by the Prophets to Paradise, to hell fire, to future reward and punishment, to have been actuated by a desire to educate and uplift the souls of men. Consider, therefore, how the generality of mankind, whatever their beliefs or theories, have recognized the excellence, and admitted the superiority, of these Prophets of God. These Gems of Detachment are acclaimed by some as the embodiments of wisdom, while others believe them to be the mouth-piece of God Himself."

This reminds us of Pascal's Wager, as depicted here[215]:

"Pascal's Wager (or Pascal's Gambit) is a suggestion posed by the French philosopher Blaise Pascal that even though the existence of God cannot be determined through reason, a person should wager as though God exists, because so living has everything to gain, and nothing to lose. It was set out in note 233 of his Pensées, a posthumously published collection of notes made by Pascal in his last years as he worked on a treatise on Christian apologetics... The wager builds on the theme of other Pensées where Pascal systematically dismantles the notion that we can trust reason, especially in the areas of religion. Although his notes were found without definite order after his death (the Pensées numbering scheme was added by publishers for reference purposes), it can be inferred that the section regarding the wager would have followed his other thoughts that supply the foundation... Pascal then asks the reader to analyze their position. If reason is truly corrupt and cannot be relied upon to decide the matter of God's existence, only a coin toss remains. In Pascal's assessment, placing a wager is unavoidable, and anyone who is incapable of trusting any evidence either for or against God's

---

[215] http://en.wikipedia.org/wiki/Pascal's_Wager

existence, must at least face the prospect that infinite happiness is at risk. The "infinite" expected value of believing is always greater than the expected value of not believing.

"However, Pascal did not treat acceptance of the wager to be in itself sufficient for salvation. In the same note where the wager is found, Pascal goes on to explain that understanding his conclusion is just the impetus for faith, not faith itself[216]: 'Endeavour then to convince yourself, not by increase of proofs of God, but by the abatement of your passions. You would like to attain faith, and do not know the way; you would like to cure yourself of unbelief, and ask the remedy for it. Learn of those who have been bound like you, and who now stake all their possessions. These are people who know the way which you would follow, and who are cured of an ill of which you would be cured. Follow the way by which they began; by acting as if they believed, bless yourself with holy water, have Masses said, and so on; by a simple and natural process this will make you believe, and will dull you—will quiet your proudly critical intellect... Now, what harm will befall you in taking this side? You will be faithful, honest, humble, grateful, generous, a sincere friend, truthful. Certainly you will not have those poisonous pleasures, glory and luxury; but will you not have others? I will tell you that you will thereby gain in this life, and that, at each step you take on this road, you will see so great certainty of gain, so much nothingness in what you risk, that you will at last recognize that you have wagered for something certain and infinite, for which you have given nothing.'"

---

[216] Blaise Pascal. *Pensées*, #233

CHAPTER FOUR

SCRIPTURAL PROOFS OF
THE EXISTENCE OF GOD

To many readers the very notion of there being traditional proofs for the existence of God to be found in the interpretations of the Scriptures of the various religions will seem preposterous. After all, you may be thinking that the Scriptures affirm the existence of a Deity, deities or no deity, but the Scriptures are not concerned with arguments in support of the existence or non-existence of such an Entity. Of course it is self-evident to any reader of the Scriptures, of the Tanakh, the Gospels, the Gathas, the Tripitaka,[217] the Bhagavad-Gita, the Qur'an and others that the texts of these Scriptures do not set forth such arguments. However, traditional proofs, while derived or abstracted from Scripture are not limited to the text of Scripture, for otherwise we would be considering proofs from Scripture.

Inasmuch as theologians and other students of Scriptures have felt the need for arguments in support of their convictions, and inasmuch as they have had to do their best to interpret the mysteries inherent in the text of their Scriptures, they have devised many such explanations and interpretations and these are the traditional proofs spoken of here. There are at least four different approaches to the deciphering of Scriptural text: 1) The first is to rely upon traditional interpretations, upon those current in one's particular denomination or sect of choice—'Abdu'l-Bahá calls

---

[217] Many Buddhists and scholars of Buddhism believe that the Buddha did not refer to God, let alone provide proofs of His existence.

this imitation of ancestral forms[218] and disdains this as a source of truth; 2) The second is to make one's own investigation and come to one's own conclusions, and this is highly approved of by divine philosophers[219]; 3) The third is to depend upon the studies of experts who claim to have deciphered what the texts of the Scriptures meant to readers when they first came into existence, and this is considered suspect by divine philosophers because of the limitations of rational enquiry and in particular of materialistic standards of research; 4) The fourth is to turn to the other Scriptures, to the Writings of the other Manifestations of God and seek to understand the meaning of the text in the light of the specific teachings of one of those Manifestations or in the same light of the general teachings of all of those Manifestations.

All of the four methods are used in the interpretation of Scripture, all but the last are considered traditional for the purposes of this study, for the last belongs to a different category of interpretation altogether, the interpretation of the prophet by the prophet. These will be considered under proofs of the Holy Spirit. A comprehensive survey of the arguments and proofs for the existence of God found in the voluminous literature of Judaism, Christianity, Islam, Hinduism, Mahayana Buddhism and the like is beyond the scope of this volume. Suffice it to say that from the very first verse to the very last, every reference to God in the Scriptures has been exhaustively studied and discussed by myriads of commentators. Even as *"we ponder each created thing, we shall witness a myriad consummate wisdoms and learn a myriad new and wondrous truths"*,[220] so also these commentators have partaken of many of the myriads of wisdoms concealed in the Holy Text. This Text however is never exhausted, for it is the Book of the Revelation of God, the Book of the Manifestation of God and the highest fruit of Divine creation. The revelation of the Book of God is of immeasurably greater difficulty and im-

---

[218] PUP 291

[219] Ibid.

[220] *Seven Valleys in The Call of the Divine Beloved*: www.bahai.org/r/871507970

portance than the creation of any of the other creations of God. Nor can this study encompass all of the various personal interpretations given to the Scriptural text by individuals in search of truth. Finally, thousands of publications have sought to clarify the sources and original meanings of Scriptural languages, and while much of this literature casts light upon the Texts, as a whole this historico-critical approach has done perhaps as much to estrange souls from discovering divine truth in Scripture as the proliferation of atheist and materialist philosophies.

It seems appropriate nonetheless to give some examples here of Scriptural proofs for the existence of God, first citing Jewish tradition, and then Roman Catholic exegesis. While this book is not altogether an interfaith study, when considering Scripture it is inevitable that some perspectives of believers will be cited. Saadia ben Fayyumi (d. 942 CE), as an eminent Jewish religious leader (Gaon of Sura), scholar and author. He is the first known Jewish exponent of proofs for the existence of God. In his Kitāb al-amānāt wa'l-I'tiqādāt (Book of Beliefs and Opinions), written in Arabic and translated during his lifetime into Hebrew, Saadia begins with discussion of the four sources of human knowledge — sensory; intuition of truth of commonsense propositions; logic; and authentic tradition. While acknowledging that God has a multiplicity of attributes, Saadia insists that this does not define God but simply give human beings the capacity to understand something about Him. His principle argument for the existence of God is an argument from design. In contrast to Saadia's focus on the implications of God's existence for the Jewish people — affirming that the perfect order of the universe requires that the Jew practice the mitzvot, whether they are understood by human reason or not — Moshe ben Maimon, known to Europeans as Maimonides and to Jews as Rambam (died 1204 CE) wrote Dalālat al-ḥā'irīn (Guide for the Perplexed), also in Arabic and also translated into Hebrew in his lifetime, in which he set forth 25 propositions to prove the existence and nature of God, in Part II of his treatise. These are two of the few treatises on the subject. Jews were so completely convinced of the reality and unity of God that it was for the most part not interesting to them to discuss the reasons for doing so.

A fine summary of the entire question of proofs for the existence of God in the Bible is found in the Roman Catholic Encyclopedia[221]:

> "Neither in the Old or New Testament do we find any elaborate argumentation devoted to proving that God exists. This truth is rather taken for granted, as being something, for example, that only the fool will deny in his heart [Ps. xiii (xiv), 1; lii (liii), 1]; and argumentation, when resorted to, is directed chiefly against polytheism and idolatry. But in several passages we have a cursory appeal to some phase of the general cosmological argument: v.g. Ps. xviii (xix), 1, xciii (xciv), 5 sqq., Is., xli, 26 sqq.; II Mach., vii, 28, etc.; and in some few others—Wis. xiii, 1–9; Rom., i, 18,20—the argument is presented in a philosophical way, and men who reason rightly are held to be inexcusable for failing to recognize and worship the one true God, the Author and Ruler of the universe.
>
> "These two latter texts merit more than passing attention. Wis., xiii, 1–9 reads: 'But all men are vain in whom there is not the knowledge of God: and who by these good things that are seen, could not understand him that is, neither by attending to the works have acknowledged who was the workman: but have imagined either the fire, or the wind, or the swift air or the circle of the stars, or the great water, or the sun and moon, to be the gods that rule the world. With whose beauty, if they, being delighted, took them to be gods: let them know how much the Lord of them is more beautiful than they: for the first author of beauty made all those things. Or if they admired their power and effects, let them un-

---

PETER TERRY �֎ PROOFS OF THE EXISTENCE OF GOD

derstand by them that he that made them, is mightier than they: for by the greatness of the beauty, and of the creature, the creator of them may be seen, so as to be known thereby. But yet as to these they are less to be blamed. For they perhaps err, seeking God, and desirous to find him. For being conversant among his works, they search: and they are persuaded that the things are good which are seen. But then again they are not to be pardoned. For if they were able to know so much as to make a judgment of the world: how did they not more easily find out the Lord thereof?'

"Here it is clearly taught

- that the phenomenal or contingent world—the things that are seen—requires a cause distinct from and greater than itself or any of its elements;

- that this cause who is God is not unknowable, but is known with certainty not only to exist but to possess in Himself, in a higher degree, whatever beauty, strength, or other perfections are realized in His works,

- that this conclusion is attainable by the right exercise of human reason, without reference to supernatural revelation, and that philosophers, therefore, who are able to interpret the world philosophically, are inexcusable for their ignorance of the true God, their failure, it is implied, being due rather to lack of good will than to the incapacity of the human mind.

"Substantially the same doctrine is laid down more briefly by St. Paul in Romans 1:18–20: 'For the wrath of God is revealed from heaven against all ungodliness and injustice of those men that detain the truth of God in injustice: because that which is known of God is manifest in them. For God hath manifested it unto them.

For the invisible things of him, from the creation of the world, are clearly seen, being understood by the things that are made, his eternal power also and divinity: so that they are inexcusable.'

"It is to be observed that the pagans of whom St. Paul is speaking are not blamed for their ignorance of supernatural revelation and the Mosaic law, but for failing to preserve or for corrupting that knowledge of God and of man's duty towards Him which nature itself ought to have taught them. Indeed it is not pure ignorance as such they are blamed for, but that willful shirking of truth which renders ignorance culpable. Even under the corruptions of paganism St. Paul recognized the indestructible permanency of germinal religious truth.[222]

"It is clear from these passages that Agnosticism and Pantheism are condemned by revelation, while the validity of the general proof of God's existence given above is confirmed. It is also clear that the extreme form of Traditionalism, which would hold that no certain knowledge of God's existence or nature is attainable by human reason without the aid of supernatural revelation, is condemned."

---

[222] cf. Romans 2:14–15

CHAPTER FIVE

SPIRITUAL PROOFS OF
THE EXISTENCE OF GOD

FIRST PROOF: IMAGE OF GOD IS PROOF OF GOD

There is man, and man is created in the image of God, therefore God exists. This may appear at first to be a circular argument, and hence one that is without foundation. It may also seem to be purely based on tradition, that is, on an interpretation of some Scriptural verses. This however is also a rational proof in an ingenious fashion. Inasmuch as man is established to be real, and as all are agreed that man holds within himself the potentiality to be, to become or to perceive infinitude; and as all that man can be, become and perceive is himself; and as that self of man is a reflection of the spiritual qualities which also exist in all things; and as the highest existence of those spiritual qualities is called by men God; therefore man reflects the reality of God, and man is the proof of the existence of God.

This is called a spiritual proof because it is described in mystical tracts, in descriptions of the mystical search, the spiritual journey. We find it in a commentary on the path of spiritual enlightenment called Chahar Vadi[223] by Bahá'u'lláh, where this proof is related to a particular station of the mystic traveler:

> "this plane pertaineth to the self—but the self which is intended is 'the Self of God that pervadeth all His laws'. In this station the self is not rejected but beloved..."[224]

---

[223] Bahá'u'lláh. *Four Valleys,* see footnotes #95
[224] Ibid.

Furthermore,

> "This station hath myriad signs and countless tokens. Hence it is said: 'We will surely show them Our signs in the world and within themselves, until it become plain to them that there is no God save Him.' One must, then, read the book of one's own self, rather than the treatise of some grammarian."[225]

This proof is articulated in Bahá'u'lláh's Lawh-i-Muhammad 'Ali with somewhat different terminology:

> "Know, verily, that the soul is the sign of God, a heavenly gem whose reality the most learned of men hath failed to grasp, and whose mystery no mind, however acute, can ever hope to unravel. It is the first among all created things to declare the excellence of its Creator, the first to recognize His glory, to cleave to His truth, and to bow down in adoration before Him. If it be faithful to God, it will reflect His light, and will, eventually, return unto Him. If it fail, however, in its allegiance to its Creator, it will become a victim to self and passion, and will, in the end, sink in their depths... Verily I say, the human soul is, in its essence, one of the signs of God, a mystery among His mysteries. It is one of the mighty signs of the Almighty, the harbinger that proclaimeth the reality of all the worlds of God. Within it lieth concealed that which the world is now utterly incapable of apprehending. Ponder in thine heart the revelation of the Soul of God that pervadeth all His Laws, and contrast it with that base and appetitive nature that hath rebelled against Him, that forbiddeth men to turn unto the Lord of Names, and impelleth them to walk after their lusts and wickedness."[226]

---

[225] Ibid.
[226] GL 158–159, 160–161

'Abdu'l-Bahá explores this theme from its inverse, that is defining the nature of man according to the nature of God. We may take this formulation and turn it inside out and see therein a statement of this spiritual proof:

> "The arguments we have adduced thus far for the originality of the human species have been rational ones. Now we will provide spiritual arguments, which are indeed the fundamental ones."[227]

> "Now, the world of existence, indeed every created thing, proclaims but one of the names of God, but the reality of man is an all-encompassing and universal reality which is the seat of the revelation of all the divine perfections. That is, a sign of each one of the names, attributes, and perfections that we ascribe to God exists in man. If such were not the case, he would be unable to imagine and comprehend these perfections. For example, we say that God is all-seeing. The eye is the sign of His sight: If this faculty were lacking in man, how could we imagine the sight of God? For one born blind cannot imagine what it is to see, any more than one born deaf can imagine what it is to hear, or the lifeless what it is to be alive. Thus, the divinity of God, which is the totality of all perfections, reveals itself in the reality of man—that is, the divine Essence is the sum total of all perfections, and from this station it casts a ray of its splendour upon the human reality. In other words, the Sun of Truth is reflected in this mirror. Thus man is a perfect mirror facing the Sun of Truth and is the seat of its reflection."[228]

Man is the reflection of the Divinity of God: man exists so God must exist.

---

[227] SAQ IV:50.1
[228] SAQ IV:50.3–4

"The splendour of all the divine perfections is manifest in the reality of man, and it is for this reason that he is the vicegerent and apostle of God. If man did not exist, the universe would be without result, for the purpose of existence is the revelation of the divine perfections. We cannot say, then, that there was a time when man was not. At most we can say that there was a time when this earth did not exist, and that at the beginning man was not present upon it."[229]

Man could not exist without God, for he is the mirror of the perfections of God; and the universe would be meaningless without man.

SECOND PROOF: DREAM IS SIGN OF GOD FOR PHILOSOPHERS

The dream world is probably the most mysterious of phenomena to all men, not only in the present but as far back into the past as we are able to discern. Bahá'u'lláh writes in Surat Vafa:

"Consider thy state when asleep. Verily, I say, this phenomenon is the most mysterious of the signs of God amongst men, were they to ponder it in their hearts. Behold how the thing which thou hast seen in thy dream is, after a considerable lapse of time, fully realized. Had the world in which thou didst find thyself in thy dream been identical with the world in which thou livest, it would have been necessary for the event occurring in that dream to have transpired in this world at the very moment of its occurrence. Were it so, you yourself would have borne witness unto it. This being not the case, however, it must necessarily follow that the world in which thou livest is different and apart from that which thou hast experienced in thy dream. This latter world hath

---

[229] SAQ IV:50.4

neither beginning nor end. It would be true if thou wert to contend that this same world is, as decreed by the All-Glorious and Almighty God, within thy proper self and is wrapped up within thee. It would be equally true to maintain that thy spirit, having transcended the limitations of sleep and having stripped itself of all earthly attachment, hath, by the act of God, been made to traverse a realm which lieth hidden in the innermost reality of this world."[230]

Elsewhere, Bahá'u'lláh writes in Lawh-i-Muhammad 'Ali:

"When man is asleep, his soul can, in no wise, be said to have been inherently affected by any external object. It is not susceptible of any change in its original state or character. Any variation in its functions is to be ascribed to external causes. It is to these external influences that any variations in its environment, its understanding, and perception should be attributed."[231]

In the same "Lawh", Bahá'u'lláh writes,

"Behold how the dream thou hast dreamed is, after the lapse of many years, re-enacted before thine eyes. Consider how strange is the mystery of the world that appeareth to thee in thy dream."[232]

In Haft Vadi, Bahá'u'lláh writes of the sixth valley on the path of spiritual enlightenment: "Indeed, O brother, if we ponder each created thing, we shall witness a myriad consummate wisdoms and learn a myriad new and wondrous truths. One of the created phenomena is the dream. Behold how many secrets have been deposited therein, how many wisdoms treasured up, how many worlds concealed. Observe how thou art asleep in a dwelling, and its doors are shut; on a sudden thou findest thyself

[230] GL 152
[231] GL 160
[232] GL 162

in a far-off city, which thou enterest without moving thy feet or wearying thy body. Without taxing thine eyes, thou seest; without troubling thine ears, thou hearest; without a tongue, thou speakest. And perchance when ten years have passed, thou wilt witness in this temporal world the very things thou hast dreamt tonight.

"Now there are many wisdoms to ponder in the dream, which none but the people of this valley can comprehend in their reality. First, what is this world where without eye or ear or hand or tongue one can put all these to use? Second, how is it that in the outer world thou seest today the effect of a dream which thou didst witness in the world of sleep some ten years past? Consider the difference between these two worlds, and the mysteries they conceal, that, attended by divine confirmations, thou mayest attain unto heavenly discoveries and enter the realms of holiness.

> "God, the Most High, hath placed these signs in men so that veiled minds might not deny the mysteries of the life beyond, nor belittle that which hath been promised them. For some hold fast to reason and deny whatever reason comprehendeth not, and yet feeble minds can never grasp the reality of the stages that we have related: The universal divine Intellect alone can comprehend them."[233]

THIRD PROOF: EVERY CHANGE IN ANY THING PROVES EXISTENCE OF GOD

We have already encountered this proof among the Rational Proofs, but here it is stated by a Prophet, and hence it will also be treated as a spiritual proof, as it is susceptible also of confirmation through intuition and faith. Bahá'u'lláh writes in Lawh-i-Muhammad 'Alí,

---

[233] SV, see footnote #95

"Consider the human eye. Though it hath the faculty of perceiving all created things, yet the slightest impediment may so obstruct its vision as to deprive it of the power of discerning any object whatsoever. Magnified be the name of Him Who hath created, and is the Cause of, these causes, Who hath ordained that every change and variation in the world of being be made dependent upon them."[234] Man perceives intuitively that the cause of the impediment of his vision or of any other of his faculties is either for good or for evil. If he "feels" that the cause is evil, he may attribute it to "bad luck", to "a curse", to "a devil", to "malevolent nature". If he "feels" that the cause is good, he may attribute it to "good luck", to "a blessing", to "an angel", to "benevolent nature". The Prophet affirms what intuition and faith have directly instructed the hearts of many millions, that the Cause of these causes is God, that hence every change or variation, including this obstructive impediment is a sign of God: "Every created thing in the whole universe is but a door leading into His knowledge, a sign of His sovereignty..."[235]

FOURTH PROOF: EVERY CREATED THING IS A PROOF OF EXISTENCE OF GOD

Change and variation are in themselves signs, proofs of the existence of God. Furthermore, the things in themselves, in their beings, their essences, their existences are also signs of God.

"Every created thing in the whole universe is but a door leading into His knowledge, a sign of His sovereignty, a revelation of His names, a symbol of His majesty, a token

[234] GL 160
[235] Ibid.

of His power, a means of admittance into His straight Path..."[236]

Likewise in the Lawh Tafsir Bayt Sa'da revealed for Shaykh Salman, Bahá'u'lláh writes:

"Know thou that every created thing is a sign of the revelation of God. Each, according to its capacity, is, and will ever remain, a token of the Almighty. Inasmuch as He, the sovereign Lord of all, hath willed to reveal His sovereignty in the kingdom of names and attributes, each and every created thing hath, through the act of the Divine Will, been made a sign of His glory. So pervasive and general is this revelation that nothing whatsoever in the whole universe can be discovered that doth not reflect His splendor...Were the Hand of Divine power to divest of this high endowment all created things, the entire universe would become desolate and void."[237]

Bahá'u'lláh Prophet further defines this argument in Lawh-i-Tafsir Bayt Sa'da as follows:

"Let no one imagine that by Our assertion that all created things are the signs of the revelation of God is meant that—God forbid—all men, be they good or evil, pious or infidel, are equal in the sight of God. Nor doth it imply that the Divine Being—magnified be His name and exalted be His glory—is, under any circumstances, comparable unto men, or can, in any way, be associated with His creatures. Such an error hath been committed by certain foolish ones who, after having ascended into the heavens of their idle fancies, have interpreted Divine Unity to mean that all created things

---

[236] Ibid. These verses are of course the continuation of the previous cited passage.
[237] GL 184

are the signs of God, and that, consequently, there is no distinction whatosever between them. Some have even outstripped them by maintaining that these signs are peers and partners of God Himself. Gracious God! He, verily, is one and indivisible; one in His essence, one in His attributes. Everything besides Him is as nothing when brought face to face with the resplendent revelation of but one of His names, with no more than the faintest intimation of His glory—how much less when confronted with His own Self!"[238]

'Abdu'l-Bahá describes this spiritual proof in this language:

"all existing things are the seat of the revelation of the divine splendours; that is, the signs of the divinity of God are manifest in the realities of all things. Just as the earth is the place where the rays of the sun are reflected—meaning that the light, heat, and influence of the sun are plain and manifest in all the atoms of the earth—so too does each one of the atoms of the universe in this infinite space proclaim one of the perfections of God. Nothing is deprived of this: Each is either a sign of the mercy of God, or of His power, or His greatness, or His justice, or His sustaining providence, or His generosity, or His sight, or His hearing, or His knowledge, or His grace, and so on. Our meaning is that every existing thing is of necessity the seat of the revelation of the divine splendours; that is, the perfections of God are manifested and revealed therein. It is even as the sun which shines upon the desert, the sea, the trees, the fruits, the blossoms—upon all earthly things. Now, the world of existence, indeed every created thing, proclaims but one of the names of God..."[239]

---

[238] GL 184, 187
[239] SAQ IV:50.2–3

FIFTH PROOF: NOT EVERY SIGN OF GOD OF SAME RANK

"Furthermore, consider the signs of the revelation of God in their relation one to another. Can the sun, which is but one of these signs, be regarded as equal in rank to darkness? The one true God beareth Me witness! No man can believe it, unless he be of those whose hearts are straitened, and whose eyes have become deluded. Say: consider your own selves. Your nails and eyes are both parts of your bodies. Do ye regard them of equal rank and value? If ye say, yea; say, then: ye have indeed charged with imposture, the Lord, my God, the All-Glorious, inasmuch as ye pare the one, and cherish the other as dearly as your own life."[240]

Also cited from Lawh-i-Tafsir Bayt Sa'da,[241] this affirmation challenges the philosophical relativist to make judgments based upon common sense, and not to oppose for the sake of opposition. This is actually a corollary to a Rational Proof, but it is also a spiritual proof inasmuch as while reason may not recognize rank, may challenge or even reject rank based upon its calculations, intuition and faith understand the inviolability of rank.

"To transgress the limits of one's rank and station is, in no wise, permissible. The integrity of every rank and station must needs be preserved. By this is meant that every created thing should be viewed in the light of the station it hath been ordained to occupy..."[242]

He continues:

"He is really a believer in the Unity of God who recognizeth in each and every created thing the sign of the revelation of Him Who is the Eternal Truth, and not he

---

[240] GL 188
[241] Ibid.
[242] Ibid.

who maintaineth that the creature is indistinguishable from the Creator."[243]

SIXTH PROOF: VISIONS AND INTUITIONS

The testimonies of hundreds if not thousands of mystics and believers of Jewish, Christian, Muslim, Sikh, Hindu, Mahayana Buddhist and other faiths are evidence that the existence of God is not a matter of speculation or even of what anti-religionists call "blind faith" for many human beings—for many both in the past and in the present, the existence of God is a matter of knowledge confirmed by personal experience. In two of his talks, 'Abdu'l-Bahá discussed this question, as applied to Manifestations of God—the principle would be the same for subjective spiritual experiences related to God:

"I will not mention the miracles of Bahá'u'lláh, for the hearer might say that these are merely traditions which may or may not be true. Such, too, is the case with the Gospel, where the accounts of the miracles of Christ come down to us from the Apostles and not from other observers, and are denied by the Jews. Were I nonetheless to mention the supernatural feats of Bahá'u'lláh, they are numerous and unequivocally acknowledged in the East, even by some of the non-believers. But these accounts cannot be a decisive proof and testimony for all, since the hearer might say that they are not factually true, as the followers of other denominations also recount miracles from their leaders. For instance, Hindus recount certain miracles of Brahma. How can we know that those are false and that these are true? If these are reported accounts, so too are those; if these are widely attested, then the same holds true of those. Thus such accounts do not constitute a suffi-

---

[243] GL 189

cient proof. Of course, a miracle may be a proof for the eyewitness, but even then he might not be sure whether what he beheld was a true miracle or mere sorcery. Indeed, extraordinary feats have also been attributed to certain magicians.

"In brief, our meaning is that many marvellous things appeared from Bahá'u'lláh, but we do not recount them, for not only do they not constitute a proof and testimony for all mankind, but they are not even a decisive proof for those who witnessed them and who may ascribe them to magic.

"Moreover, most of the miracles attributed to the Prophets have an inner meaning. For instance, it is recorded in the Gospel that upon the martyrdom of Christ darkness fell, the earth shook, the veil of the Temple was rent in twain, and the dead arose from their graves. If this had outwardly come to pass, it would have been a stupendous thing. Such an event would have undoubtedly been recorded in the chronicles of the time and would have seized with dismay the hearts of men. At the very least the soldiers would have removed Christ from the cross or would have fled. But as these events have not been recorded in any history, it is evident that they are not to be understood literally but according to their inner meaning. Our purpose is not to deny, but merely to say that these accounts do not constitute a decisive proof, and that they have an inner meaning—nothing more."[244]

"For example, were a non-believing seeker to be told of the miracles of Moses and Christ, he would deny them and say: "Miracles have also long been ascribed to certain idols by the testimony of a multitude and recorded in books. Thus the Brahmans have compiled an entire book regarding the miracles of Brahma." The seeker would then ask: "How can we know that the Jews and the Christians speak the truth and that the Brahmans lie? For both are traditions, both are widely attested, and both have been recorded in a book. Each can be viewed as plausible or implausible, as with every other account: If one is true, both must be true; if one is accepted, both must be accepted." Therefore, miracles cannot be a conclusive proof, for even if they are valid proofs for those who were present, they fail to convince those who were not."[245]

SEVENTH PROOF: DIVINE REVELATION IS THE GREATEST SIGN OF GOD

In the Lawh-i-Na'mat'u'llah Bahá'u'lláh writes of the various gifts given by God to mankind, beginning with the gift of understanding, then the power of vision, then the other senses:

"That which is preeminent above all other gifts, is incorruptible in nature, and pertaineth to God Himself, is the gift of Divine Revelation. Every bounty conferred by the Creator upon man, be it material or spiritual, is subservient unto this. It is, in its essence, and will ever so remain, the Bread which cometh down from Heaven. It is God's supreme testimony, the clearest evidence of His truth, the sign of His consummate bounty, the token of His all-encompassing mercy, the proof of His most loving providence, the symbol of His most perfect grace."[246]

How can man partake of this gift? He partakes of the gifts of understanding and of the senses every moment of every waking hour. But to partake of this gift man must turn to the giver thereof.

---

[245] SAQ II:22:4
[246] GL 195

"He hath, indeed, partaken of this highest gift of God who hath recognized His Manifestation in this Day."[247]

This is also a rational proof, for if the Revelation of God through the agency of His Manifestation is His greatest and most perfect sign, the greatest proof of His reality, then it must logically follow that the Manifestation of God is the necessary vehicle of that Revelation and that recognition of the Manifestation of God is the same as partaking of the Revelation of God. It also follows that one who has partaken of this Revelation from God through recognition of the Manifestation of God is himself a sign of God on earth.

Abraham Heschel likewise designated this as one of the ways in which man encounters God, as described by George F. Thomas[248]:

"The second way to the presence of God is the revelation recorded in the Bible and preserved in tradition. While "moments of insight" awaken faith in a transcendent meaning beyond the mystery of the world, says Heschel, they do not give us knowledge that it is the "living God" or "tell us bow to live in a way that is compatible with the grandeur, the mystery, and the glory".[249] Man is in need of a definite "creed" and "way of living".[250] Therefore, we must look for guidance to the prophets through whom Cod has expressed his will to us.[251] Heschel is well aware of the resistance of modern men to the belief in a revelation from God. They find it difficult because they hold two opposed views of man. On the one hand, they

---

[247] GL 195

[248] George F. Thomas. "Philosophy and theology," *Theology Today, 30* (3), 1973, pp. 274–275. Retrieved October 2004, from http://theologytoday. ptsem.edu/oct1973/v30–3-article8.htm.

[249] Abraham Joshua Heschel. *God in Search of Man.* New York: Jewish Publishing Society, 1955, p. 163

[250] Ibid.

[251] Ibid., p. 164

regard man as self-sufficient, "too great to be in need of divine guidance," confident that technology can solve all problems and social reform can eliminate all evils.[252] Or they view him as "insignificantly small in relation to the universe" and cannot believe that "the infinite spirit should come down to commune with the feeble, finite mind of man".[253]

"Heschel points out that man, who possesses both the ability to create and the power to destroy, is important enough to God to receive spiritual light from God to guide him.[254] Moreover, those who have experienced moments of insight into a transcendent meaning themselves, he says, "will not feel alien to the [prophetic] minds that received not a spark [of illumination] but a flame".[255] However, Heschel realizes that behind this resistance to belief in revelation is the modem naturalistic world view which regards history no less than nature as an impersonal and uniform process of causes and effects which is subject to no intervention from beyond itself. To this world view he opposes the biblical belief that God is the source of the whole system of natural laws, transcends it by his freedom, and through his revelation of himself introduces a "new creative moment into the course of history".[256] Thus, the Bible is a record of the revelation of God through unique and unrepeatable events of history. Here, as in his view of man as a spiritual being capable of devoting himself to universal ends, Heschel shows himself to be an uncompromising critic of modern naturalism."

---

[252] Ibid., p. 169
[253] Ibid., p. 170
[254] Ibid., p. 171
[255] Ibid., p. 174
[256] Ibid., p. 211

EIGHTH PROOF: MANIFESTATION OF GOD IS GREATEST SIGN OF GOD

As it has already been affirmed, the Revelation of God is the greatest gift of God to man and also the greatest sign of God upon the earth. This is stated first of all in reference to all of the Manifestations of God:

> "Wert thou to ponder in thine heart the behavior of the Prophets of God thou wouldst assuredly and readily testify that there must needs be other worlds besides this world...Consider, therefore, how the generality of mankind, whatever their beliefs or theories, have recognized the excellence, and admitted the superiority, of these Prophets of God. These Gems of Detachment are acclaimed by some as the embodiments of wisdom, while others believe them to be the mouthpiece of God Himself. How could such Souls have consented to surrender themselves unto their enemies if they believed all the worlds of God to have been reduced to this earthly life? Would they have willingly suffered such afflictions and torments as no man hath ever experienced or witnessed?"[257]

The way for man to partake of this greatest gift is through the recognition of His current Manifestation:

> "He hath, indeed partaken of this highest gift of God who hath recognized His Manifestation in this Day."[258]

So writes Bahá'u'lláh in the Lawh-i-Na'mat'u'lláh. In another "Lawh" is written:

> "The essence of belief in Divine unity consisteth in regarding Him Who is the Manifestation of God and Him Who is the invisible, the inaccessible, the unknowable

---

[257] GL 157–158
[258] GL 195

> Essence as one and the same. By this is meant that what-
> ever pertaineth to the former, all His acts and doings,
> whatever He ordaineth or forbiddeth, should be consid-
> ered, in all their aspects, and under all circumstances,
> and without any reservation, as identical with the Will
> of God Himself. This is the loftiest station to which a
> true believer in the unity of God can ever hope to attain.
> Blessed is the man that reacheth this station, and is of
> them that are steadfast in their belief."[259]

'Abdu'l-Bahá states similarly the relationship between knowledge of God and knowledge of the Manifestation of God:

> "The knowledge of the reality of the Divinity is in no
> wise possible, but the knowledge of the Manifestations
> of God is the knowledge of God, for the bounties, splen-
> dours, and attributes of God are manifest in Them. Thus,
> whoso attains to the knowledge of the Manifestations
> of God attains to the knowledge of God, and whoso re-
> mains heedless of Them remains bereft of that knowl-
> edge."[260]

NINTH PROOF: BELIEVER IS ONE OF THE SIGNS OF GOD

As the Revelation of God is the greatest sign of God, and
the Manifestation of God is the appearance of that Revelation,
so then the believer in the Revelation and the Manifestation of
God is in himself a mighty sign of God, a proof of the existence of
God par excellence. In the Lawh-i-Muhammad 'Ali, Bahá'u'lláh
writes:

> "Whoso hath, in this Day, refused to allow the doubts
> and fancies of men to turn him away from Him Who is
> the Eternal Truth, and hath not suffered the tumult

---

[259] GL 167
[260] SAQ IV:59.9

provoked by the ecclesiastical and secular authorities to deter him from recognizing His Message, such a man will be regarded by God, the Lord of all men, as one of His mighty signs, and will be numbered among them whose names have been inscribed by the Pen of the Most High in His Book."[261]

'Abdu'l-Bahá, after establishing that *"whoso attains to the knowledge of the Manifestations of God attains to the knowledge of God"*[262] continues with

"We cherish the hope that the loved ones of God, like unto an attractive force, will draw these bounties from their very source and arise with such radiance and exert such influence as to become the perspicuous signs of the Sun of Truth."[263]

TENTH PROOF: PERFECTED PROOF OF GOD IN THIS DAY

The Revelation of God is the greatest proof of the existence of God for man, and the Manifestation of God, being the appearance of that Revelation is the most perfect and perceptible form of that proof. But Bahá'u'lláh takes this proof even further:

"I testify, O my God, that this is the Day whereon Thy TESTIMONY hath been fulfilled, and Thy clear TOKENS have been manifested, and Thine UTTERANCES have been revealed, and Thy SIGNS have been demonstrated, and the radiance of Thy COUNTENANCE hath been diffused, and Thy PROOF HATH BEEN PERFECTED, and Thine ASCENDANCY hath been established, and Thy MERCY hath overflowed, and the Day Star of Thy GRACE hath shone forth with such brilliance that Thou didst mani-

---

[261] GL 159
[262] SAQ IV:59.9
[263] Ibid.

fest Him Who is the Revealer of Thyself and the Treasury of Thy wisdom and the Dawning-Place of Thy majesty and power."[264]

Lest there be any confusion regarding the meaning of this passage, in another passage Bahá'u'lláh writes:

"I entreat Thee, by Thy Most Great Name, Whom Thou hast appointed as the unerring Balance among the nations, and Thine INFALLIBLE PROOF unto all men, not to forsake me, nor to abandon me to my corrupt desires."

The Most Great Name is a reference to Bahá'u'lláh. Bahá'u'lláh also refers to "infallible proofs" in Kitab-i-Iqan,[265] in writing about the Day and Manifestation of the Primal Point, Siyyid 'Ali Muhammad Shirazi (the Bab):

"Having thus demonstrated that no day is greater than this Day, and no revelation more glorious than this Revelation, and having set forth all these weighty and INFALLIBLE PROOFS which no understanding mind can question, and no man of learning overlook, how can man possibly, through the idle contention of the people of doubt and fancy, deprive himself of such a bountiful grace?"[266]

In another passage in that same epistle, Bahá'u'lláh refers to the believers in the prophet of God in every Age:

"They that valiantly labour in quest of God's will, when once they have renounced all else but Him, will be so attached and wedded to that City that a moment's separation from it would to them be unthinkable. They will hearken unto INFALLIBLE PROOFS from the Hyacinth of that assembly, and receive the SUREST TESTIMONIES

[264] P&M 35–36; BWF:82
[265] KI 143–144
[266] P&M 100

from the beauty of its Rose and the melody of its Nightingale."[267]

It is evident that the "infallible proofs" to which Bahá'u'lláh refers in the Kitab-i-Iqan are proofs of the existence of Manifestations of God, for each Manifestation will reveal "infallible proofs" of His Truth. How then are these "infallible proofs" also proofs of the existence of God? What we know of the reality of God is whatever has been revealed to us by the Manifestations of God, and consequently, the only "infallible proof" for the existence of God is the proof revealed by the Manifestation of God. Man does not know God except through the Manifestation of God and therefore the only "infallible proof" of God is one that is revealed to man by the Manifestation. The meaning then of this spiritual proof is that the only completely reliable proof of the existence of God is that proof revealed by the Manifestation of God, and according to Bahá'u'lláh, this "infallible proof" has been perfected in this Day, through the divine revelation of Twin Manifestations.[268]

---

[267] KI 198–199

[268] For more information about the Twin Manifestations please look for the author's series of books on the Proofs of Prophethood.

BIBLIOGRAPHY

'Abdu'l-Bahá, 1918. *'Abdu'l-Bahá on Divine Philosophy*, edited by Isabel Fraser Chamberlain. Boston: Tudor Press.

———, 1923. *Bahá'í Scriptures*, edited by Horace Holley. New York: Brentano's.

———, 1943/1956. *Bahá'í World Faith*, edited by Horace Holley. Wilmette: Bahá'í Publishing Trust.

———, 1922/2007. *The Promulgation of Universal Peace*, edited by Howard MacNutt. Wilmette: Bahá'í Publishing Trust.

———, 1908/2014. *Some Answered Questions*, edited by Laura Clifford Barney, revised by Bahá'í World Centre. Haifa: BWC

———, 1875/1957. *The Secret of Divine Civilization*.Wilmette: Bahá'í Publishing Trust

———, 2010. *Selections from the Writings of 'Abdu'l-Bahá*. Wilmette: Bahá'í Publishing

———,1913, 1915, 1919, 1923. *Star of the West*, VI:3,8; X:10; XIV:4. Chicago: Bahá'í Publishing Society

———, n.d./1981. *Tablet of 'Abdu'l-Bahá*, in *Bahiyyih Nakhjavani, Response*. Oxford: George Ronald

———,1915, 1919. *Tablets of 'Abdu'l-Bahá*, I–III. Chicago: Bahá'í Publishing Society

Anselm of Canterbury, 1076. *The Monologion*

Aristotle, 384–322 BCE. *The Physics*; Fragment

Aquinas, Thomas, 1570. *Summa Theologiae*

Bahá'u'lláh, 1854/2018. *Four Valleys, in The Call of the Divine Beloved*. Haifa: Bahá'í World Centre

———, 1854/2018. *Seven Valleys, in The Call of the Divine Beloved*. Haifa: Bahá'í World Centre

———, 1862/1989. *Kitab-i-Iqan*. Wilmette: Bahá'í Publishing Trust

————, n.d./1988. *Gleanings from the Writings of Bahá'u'lláh.* Wilmette: Bahá'í Publishing Trust

————, 1857/1998. *Hidden Words* (Arabic). Wilmette: Bahá'í Publishing Trust

————, ca. 1880/1988. *Lawh-i-Hikmat,* Tablets of Bahá'u'lláh revealed after the Kitab-i-Aqdas. Wilmette: Bahá'í Publishing Trust

Davidson, Herbert A., 1987. *Proofs for Eternity, Creation and the Existence of God in Medieval Islamic and Jewish Philosophy.* New York: Oxford University Press.

Descartes, Rene, 1641. *Meditations*

————, 1644. *Principles of Philosophy*

Finch, Ida A. and Knobloch, Alma and Fanny H. *Flowers culled from the Rose Garden of Acca.* n.p.

Hatcher, William S., 1994. "A Scientific Proof of the Existence of God," *The Journal of Bahá'í Studies,* IV:5

————, 1996. "Prologue Proving God"; "Causality, Composition, and the Origin of Existence"; "A Scientific Proof of the Existence of God", in *The Law of Love Enshrined: Selected Essays.* Oxford: George Ronald

Heschel, Abraham Joshua, 1955. *God in Search of Man.* New York: Jewish Publishing Society

Mill, John Stuart, 1874. *Nature and the Utility of Religion*

Paul, 55 CE. *Epistle to the Romans.* New Testament

Plato, 380 BCE. *Republic*

Thomas, George F., 1973. "Philosophy and Theology," *Theology Today,* 30(3)

Oxford Universal Dictionary on Historical Principles, 3rd edition. Oxford: Clarendon Press, 1955

The International Cyclopedia. New York: Dodd & Mead Co., 1898

APPENDIX

SUGGESTIONS FOR FURTHER READING

Adams, R., 1971. "The Logical Structure of Anselm's Argument", *Philosophical Review* 80: 28–54

———, 1988. "Presumption and the Necessary Existence of God" *Nous* 22: 19–34

———, 1995a. *Leibniz: Determinist, Theist, Idealist.* Oxford: Oxford University Press

———, 1995b. "Introductory Note to *1970" in K. Gödel Collected Works Volume III: *Unpublished essays and lectures* (editor-in-chief Solomon Feferman). New York: Oxford University Press, pp.388–402

Alston, W. 1960. "The Ontological Argument Revisited" *Philosophical Review* 69: 452–74

Anderson, C., 1990. "Some Emendations on Gödel's Ontological Proof". *Faith and Philosophy* 7: 291–303

Anselm, St., *Proslogion*, in St. Anselm's Proslogion, M. Charlesworth (ed.), Oxford: OUP, 1965 [http://www.fordham.edu/halsall/source/anselm.html, in the Internet Medieval Sourcebook, Paul Halsall (ed.), Fordham University Center for Medieval Studies, translation by David Burr]

Aquinas, St. Thomas. *Summa Theologica*, Part I Q.2, article 3, literally translated by Fathers of the English Dominican Province, London: Burn, Oates & Washbourne, 1920 [http://www.fordham.edu/halsall/source/aquinas1.html, in the Internet Medieval Sourcebook, Paul Halsall (ed.), Fordham University Center for Medieval Studies, translation by David Burr]

Aristotle. *Physics* 267a-b. *Metaphysics* 994a-b, 1071b-1073a.

Ayer, A. *Language, Truth and Logic,* second edition. London: Gollancz, 1948

Barnes, J., 1972. *The Ontological Argument.* London: Macmillan

Campbell, R., 1976. From *Belief to Understanding.* Canberra: ANU Press

Chambers, T., 2000. *On Behalf of the Devil: A Parody of St. Anselm Revisited. Proceedings of the Aristotelian Society.* New Series—Volume C: 93–113

Chandler, H., 1993. "Some Ontological Arguments" *Faith and Philosophy* 10: 18–32

Charlesworth, M., 1965. *Anselm's Proslogion.* Oxford: Oxford University Press

Copleston, Frederick. *A History of Philosophy,* vol. 1, pp. 312–319. Section on the Aristotle's metaphysics and the unmoved mover.

Craig, William Lane. *The Cosmological Argument from Newton to Leibniz.* New York: Barnes and Noble, 1980.

Davidson, Herbert, 1987. *Proofs for Eternity, Creation and the Existence of God in Medieval Islamic and Jewish Philosophy.* Oxford University Press, 1987.

Descartes, R. *Discourse on Method and The Meditations,* translated with an introduction by F. Sutcliffe, Harmondsworth.Penguin, 1968 [Translation of The Meditations, by John Veitch, LL.D., available online]

Dummett, M., 1993. "Existence". *In The Seas of Language.* Oxford: Oxford University Press

Encyclopedia of Philosophy. New York: Macmillan, 1967. Various articles listed under "God, Arguments for the Existence of".

Findlay, J., 1949. "Can God's Existence Be Disproved?" *Mind* 57: 176–83

Frege, G. *Die Grundlagen der Arithmetik.* Bresnau: Koebner, 1884; translated as The Foundations of Arithmetic, J. L. Austin (trans). Oxford: Blackwell, 1974, 2nd rev edition.

Gaskin, J.C.A. "Philosophy and the Existence of God". In *An Encyclopedia of Philosophy.* G.H.R. Parkinson, ed. London: Routledge, 1988. Overview of principal proofs.

Gaunilo. "On Behalf of the Fool", in *St. Anselm's Proslogion.* M. Charlesworth (ed.). Oxford: OUP, 1965 [http://www.fordham.edu/halsall/source/anselm.html, in the Internet Medieval Sourcebook, Paul Halsall (ed.), Fordham University Center for Medieval Studies, translation by David Burr]

Gilsinan, K. (2004, February 17). "Does God exist? Yes, mathematician says." *Columbia Spectator.* Retrieved October 2004, from http://www.columbiaspectator.com/vnews/display.v/ART/2004/02/17/4031d9166ab57

Grey, W., 2000. "Gasking's Proof" *Analysis* 60:368–370

Hartshorne, C., 1965. *Anselm's Discovery: A Re-Examination of the Ontological Proof for God's Existence.* La Salle, Ill: Open Court

Hatcher, William. *Logic and Logos,* ch. 3, "From Metaphysics to Logic", pp. 60–80. Analysis of Avicenna's cosmological proof, and a modern set theoretical formulation.

———, "A Scientific Proof for the Existence of God", *Journal of Bahá'í Studies,* vol. 5, no. 4, pp. 1–16. Introduces the argument from thermodynamics and evolution.

Hatcher, William, and **Hatcher, John.** *The Law of Love Enshrined.* Oxford: George Ronald, 1996. Contains an updated version of the Logic and Logos article and a "prologue on proving God".

Hazen, A., 1999. "On Gödel's Ontological Proof". *Australasian Journal of Philosophy* 76: 361–377

Hegel, G. "The Ontological Proof According to the Lectures of 1831," in P. Hodgson (ed.). *Lectures on the Philosophy of Religion,* Vol. III. Berkeley: University of California Press, 1985, pp.351–8

Henle, P., 1961. "Uses of the Ontological Argument". *Philosophical Review* 70: 102–9

Holt, T. (2004). "Arguments for the existence of God." *Philosophy of Religion.* Retrieved October 2004, from http://www.philosophyofreligion.info/theisticproofs.html.

Hume, D. *Dialogues Concerning Natural Religion,* 1779. edited with an introduction by H. Aiken. London: Macmillan, 1948 [Electronic version, edited by James Fieser, available online]

Johnston, M., 1992. "Explanation, Response-Dependence, and Judgement-Dependence". In P. Menzies, ed., *Response-Dependent Concepts. Working Papers in Philosophy*, RSSS, ANU, 123–83

Jones, R. (2003). *Philosophy and the proof of the existence of God.* Retrieved October 2004, from http://www.philosopher.org.uk/god.htm

Kant, I. *Critique of Pure Reason*, 1787. Second edition, translated by N. Kemp-Smith. London: Macmillan, 1933

La Croix, R., 1972. *Proslogion II and III: A Third Interpretation of Anselm's Argument.* Leiden: Brill

Leibniz, G. *New Essay Concerning Human Understanding*, 1709, translated by A. Langley. New York: Macmillan, 1896

Lewis, D., 1970. "Anselm and Actuality", *Nous* 4: 175–88

Malcolm, N., 1960. "Anselm's Ontological Arguments" *Philo-sophical Review* 69: 41–62

Mann, W., 1972. "The Ontological Presuppositions of the Ontological Argument", *Review of Metaphysics* 26: 260–77

Musavi Lari, M. (n.d.). *Perfecting man's faith and conviction* (Chapter 1). Knowing God. [trans. F.J. Goulding]. Retrieved October 2004, from http://home.swipnet.se/islam/books/knowing_god/knowing_god.htm

Oppenheimer, P., and Zalta, E., 1991. "On the Logic of the Ontological Argument" in J. Tomberlin (ed.) *Philosophical Perspectives* 5: The Philosophy of Religion. Atascadero: Ridgeview: 509–29 [Preprint available online]

Oppy, G., 1995. *Ontological Arguments and Belief in God.* New York: Cambridge University Press

Oppy, G., 1996. "Gödelian Ontological Arguments". *Analysis* 56: 226–230

Oppy, G., 2000. "Response to Gettings". *Analysis* 60: 363–367

Oppy, G., 2003. Winter. "Ontological arguments" in E. Zalta (Ed.), *Stanford Encyclopedia of Philosophy.* Retrieved October 2004, from http://plato.stanford.edu/entries/ontological-arguments/.

Plantinga, A., ed. *The Ontological Argument from St. Anselm to Contemporary Philosophers.* Garden City, N.Y.: Anchor Books, 1965.

Contains St. Anselm's original formulation of the ontological argument and subsequent critiques and reformulations.

———, 1967. *God and Other Minds*. Ithaca: Cornell University Press

———, 1974. *The Nature of Necessity*. Oxford: Oxford University Press

Rescher, N., 1959. "The Ontological Proof Revisited". *Austral-asian Journal of Philosophy* 37: 138–48

Ross, J., 1969. *Philosophical Theology*. New York: Bobbs-Merrill

Rowe, W., 1989. "The Ontological Argument" in J. Feinberg (ed.) *Reason and Responsibility*, seventh edition. Belmont, CA: Wadsworth, pp. 8–17

Salmon, N., 1987. "Existence" in J. Tomberlin (ed.) *Philosophical Perspectives* 1: Metaphysics. Atascadero, CA: Ridgeview: 49–108

Smart, J., 1955. "The Existence of God" in A. Flew and A. MacIntyre (eds.) *New Essays in Philosophical Theology*. London: SCM Press: 500–509

Sobel, J., 1987. "Gödel's Ontological Proof". In *On Being and Saying: Essays for Richard Cartwright*, ed. J. Thomson. Cambridge, Mass: MIT Press, pp. 241–61

———, 2004. *Logic and Theism*. New York: Cambridge Univer-sity Press.

Spinoza, B. *The Ethics*, 1677, translation of 1883 by R. Elwes. New York: Dover, 1955 [http://frank.mtsu.edu/~rbombard/RB/Spinoza/ethica-front.html, prepared by R. Bombardi, for the Philosophy Web Works project, Middle Tennessee State Univerity]

Tooley, M., 1981. "Plantinga's Defence of the Ontological Argument" *Mind* 90: 422–7

Van Inwagen, P., 1977. "Ontological Arguments" *Nous* 11: 375–395

ALSO BY THIS AUTHOR

Books

The Archeology of the Kingdom of God. *Translation of Jean-Marc Lepain's "L'Archeologie du Royaume de Dieu."*
Bahá'í Studies in Europe.
Companion to Proofs of the Prophets.
Proofs of the Prophets.
Proofs of the Prophets. *The Case for Lord Krishna.*
Proofs of the Prophets. *The Case for Bahá'u'lláh.*
A Prophet in Modern Times. *Annotated translation of chapters from A.L.M. Nicolas "Seyyed Ali Mohammed dit le Báb."*

Articles

'Abdu'l-Bahá on Pantheism.
'Abdu'l-Bahá's Explanation of the Teachings of Bahá'u'lláh Tablets and Talks Translated into English (1911–1920).
All Abide by His Bidding: The Universal Law of God. *On the liberty of the individual vis-à-vis the laws of God guiding people to making the "right" choices.*
Bahá'í Faith in America as Panopticon 1963–1997, by Juan Cole: The Myth of the Objective Observer. *Book Review.*
Bahá'í Epistemology. *Statements of Abdu'l-Bahá on the four modes of knowledge: sense perception, reason, tradition, and inspiration. All must defer to the divine standard.*
Bahá'í Faith in America, by William Garlington: Review, by Peter Terry. *Book Review.*
Bahá'í Hermeneutics: An Academic and Primary Source Inquiry, by Peter Terry. *An exploration of the practice of scriptural interpretation by contrasting the "normative" approaches of the*

Central Figures with contemporary scholastic approaches by Juan Cole, Christopher Buck, Dann May, Michael Sours, Jack McLean, and Sen McGlinn.

Bahá'u'lláh and the Reconciliation of Religions. *The reconciliation of religions is one of the principal themes of Bahá'u'lláh's writings, yet one rarely discussed in introductions to the Bahá'í Faith and often ignored in surveys of Bahá'í teachings.*

Before Abraham was, I am. *Some Chronological Issues in the Lawh-i-Hikmat of Bahá'u'lláh.*

Concealment and Burial of the Báb, in A Most Noble Pattern: Collected Essays on the Writings of the Báb, edited by Todd Lawson and Omid Ghaemmagami. *This chapter from A.-L.-M. Nicolas' seminal biography Seyyed Ali Mohammed dit le Báb (1905) tells the story of the death and burial of the Bab, compiled from the reports of several eye-witnesses consulted by the author.*

The Covenant: Brit Olam. *The concept of covenant is found in the Bible, the Qur'an, and Bahá'í writings. Using the form of an inter-religious dialogue, this paper correlates references to covenant in four religions, demonstrating the distinctive characteristics of each.*

Dialogue on Infallibility: A response to Udo Schaefer's 'Infallible Institutions?' *An extended review of the themes first published in Schaefer's "Making the Crooked Straight," presented in the form of a dialogue. Part of this paper was delivered at the Association for Bahá'í Studies conference in 2006.*

Essays on Jesus and the New Testament. *Scripture and progressive revelation, canonization of the Bible, teachings of the New Testament, Bahá'í interpretations of the Bible, Apostles of Jesus, and prophecies of Jesus and their fulfillment. Prepared for the Wilmette Institute.*

Henrietta Emogene Martin Hoagg: Short Biographical Monograph. *Biography of a travel-teacher, translator of the Writings into Italian, and the first pioneer to Italy. She had a great impact on her fellow believers during her lifetime, but is little-recognized today.*

The Last Words of Jesus.

Marian Crist Lippitt: Short Biographical Monograph. *Controversial both during her lifetime and after, Lippitt was a trained engineer who applied her rigorous intellect to the study of metaphysics and epistemology, and is best known for developing an education philosophy titled "The Science of Reality."*

The Messiah Returns.

Persian Bayán: Summary and Thematic Analysis. *A detailed overview of this lengthy text of The Báb, which outlines elements of Bábí law, discussion of religious concepts, and the glorification of "He whom God shall make manifest."*

The Purposes and Objectives of Bahá'í Scholarship: Compilation and commentary. *Three essays on objectives of Bahá'í Scholarship, attaining to the knowledge of God, and the study of philosophy.*

Qourrèt-oul-Aíne [Qurratu'l-'Ayn], by A.L.M. Nicolas, in Tahirih in History: Perspectives on Qurratu'l-'Ayn from East and West, ed. Sabir Afaqi (2004). *First publication in English translation of early accounts of the life and death of Táhirih. These passages are from Seyyed Ali Mohammad dit le Bab (1905) by A.-L.-M. Nicolas, French diplomat and author.*

Qur'an 9:30—Messiah and the Son of God.

Qur'an 9:30—Ezra as the Son of God.

Rabindranath Tagore: Some Encounters with Bahá'ís. *'Abdu'l-Bahá is alleged to have met India's poet laureate Tagore in Chicago in 1912. This article examines the historical sources for that story, and of Martha Root's visit to Tagore's university, and the author's visit and discovery of a hitherto unknown letter.*

The Reconciliation of Religions: Imperative for the 21st Century. *While the 12 principles attributed to 'Abdu'l-Bahá include the harmony of religion with science and reason and the imperative that religion lead to unity, one principle that was at least as prominent is often left out: the reconciliation of religions.*

The Sovereign Remedy: A Study of Bahá'í Sources. *Quotations showing that Baha'u'lláh and his authoritative interpreters state what fundamentalists of many faiths have been saying for centuries: that God's guidance revealed to humanity provides the best remedy for all human ills.*

Tablet Concerning the Day of the Martyrdom of His Holiness, the Exalted One: Le Tablette Concernant l'Anniversaire du Martyre de Sa Sainteté, Exaltée, by 'Abdu'l-Bahá, in Ayyam-i-Tis'ih [The Nine Days] (1981). *Three translations: a French version by Rochan Mavaddat, an English rendering by Peter Terry, and an English translation from the original Persian by Khazeh Fananapazir.*

The Tablet of All Food: The Hierarchy of the Spiritual Worlds and the Metaphoric Nature of Physical Reality, by Jean-Marc Lepain. *English rendering in Bahá'í Studies Review, 16 (2010).*

The Three Blasphemies. *A Bahá'í Interpretation.*

Truth Triumphs: A Bahá'í Response to Misrepresentations of the Bahá'í Teachings and Bahá'í History. *Rebuttal of Francis Beckwith's thesis "Bahá'í, A Christian response to Bahá'ísm, the religion which aims toward one world government and one common faith."*

Made in the USA
Middletown, DE
21 August 2019